WRITINGS FROM THE GOLDEN AGE OF RUSSIAN POETRY

RUSSIAN LIBRARY

R

The Russian Library at Columbia University Press publishes an expansive selection of Russian literature in English translation, concentrating on works previously unavailable in English and those ripe for new translations. Works of premodern, modern, and contemporary literature are featured, including recent writing. The series seeks to demonstrate the breadth, surprising variety, and global importance of the Russian literary tradition and includes not only novels but also short stories, plays, poetry, memoirs, creative nonfiction, and works of mixed or fluid genre.

Editorial Board:

Vsevolod Bagno	Dmitry Bak
Rosamund Bartlett	Caryl Emerson
Peter B. Kaufman	Mark Lipovetsky
Oliver Ready	Stephanie Sandler

■ □ ■

Between Dog and Wolf by Sasha Sokolov, translated by
    Alexander Boguslawski
Strolls with Pushkin by Andrei Sinyavsky, translated by
    Catharine Theimer Nepomnyashchy and Slava I. Yastremski
Fourteen Little Red Huts and Other Plays by Andrei Platonov,
    translated by Robert Chandler, Jesse Irwin, and Susan Larsen
Rapture: A Novel by Iliazd, translated by Thomas J. Kitson
City Folk and Country Folk by Sofia Khvoshchinskaya, translated
    by Nora Seligman Favorov

WRITINGS FROM

THE GOLDEN AGE OF

RUSSIAN POETRY

Presented &
translated by
Peter France

KONSTANTIN
BATYUSHKOV

Columbia University Press *New York*

Columbia University Press
Publishers Since 1893
New York   Chichester, West Sussex
cup.columbia.edu

Published with the support of Read Russia, Inc.,
    and the Institute of Literary Translation, Russia

Library of Congress Cataloging-in-Publication Data
Names: Batyushkov, K. N. (Konstantin Nikolaevich), 1787–1855,
    author. | France, Peter, 1935– translator.
Title: Writings from the Golden Age of Russian poetry / Konstantin
    Batyushkov; presented and translated by Peter France.
Description: New York : Columbia University Press, 2017. | Series:
    Russian library | Includes index.
Identifiers: LCCN 2017015324 (print) | LCCN 2017019738 (ebook) |
    ISBN 9780231546140 (electronic) | ISBN 9780231185400 (cloth :
    alk. paper) | ISBN 9780231185417 (pbk.)
Classification: LCC PG3321.B4 (ebook) | LCC PG3321.B4 A2 2017
    (print) | DDC 891.78/309—dc23
LC record available at https://lccn.loc.gov/2017015324

Cover design: Roberto de Vicq de Cumptich
Book design: Lisa Hamm

CONTENTS

PREFACE

Surprisingly little pre-twentieth-century Russian poetry is readily available and well known in the English-speaking world—Pushkin, Lermontov, perhaps Tyutchev, but hardly any other poets. Yet there is a rich poetic world here, particularly from the early decades of the nineteenth century, the time of the so-called Pushkin Pléiade. The great names include Evgeny Baratynsky, Vasily Zhukovsky, Pyotr Vyazemsky, and the poet to whom this volume is devoted, Konstantin Batyushkov.

I have been living with Batyushkov, one way or another, for some time now. It was decades ago that I first read him—the moving elegy entitled "Shade of a Friend," which figures with two other poems by him in Dmitry Obolensky's pathbreaking *Penguin Book of Russian Verse*. The poems are accompanied by good prose translations, but I felt the urge to attempt a verse translation. Not long afterward I first read (and then translated) the poem by Gennady Aygi, "House of the Poet in Vologda" (1966), which concludes the present volume—in this I found a haunting image of a vulnerable poet who succumbed to madness. Later I discovered a poem written some thirty-five years earlier, the poem by Osip Mandelstam that opens this book, and realized how important Batyushkov was for the greatest of twentieth-century Russian poets. Continuing to translate him, I came to feel that this was a poet who should be more widely known in the English-speaking world, the more so because his writing echoed his involvement in some of the great events of modern European history. My aim in writing this book has been to situate his work in relation to his life experience at a crucial time in the development of modern Russian culture. The translations of his poetry are central to this book (and are discussed in a translator's note at the end of the volume); in what follows they are interwoven with his prose writings and letters to create a narrative of his fascinating and troubled life.

ACKNOWLEDGMENTS

I am particularly indebted to Vyacheslav Koshelev's *Konstantin Batyushkov: Stranstviya i strasti* (Konstantin Batyushkov: Wandering and Passions), a sympathetic and richly documented biography of the poet, and have also read with much profit what seems to be the only book-length study of Batyushkov in English, the literary-historical essay *Konstantin Batyushkov* by the Russian scholar Ilya Z. Serman (New York: Twayne, 1974). See also a detailed biographical sketch by Igor A. Pilshchikov and T. Henry Fitt, "Konstantin Batiushkov: Life and Work," www.rvb.ru/batyushkov/bio/bio_eng.htm.

All translations from Russian, both the prose and the verse, are my own. Earlier versions of some of the verse appeared in the following publications: *European Romantic Poetry*, edited by Michael Ferber; *The Penguin Book of Russian Poetry*, edited by Robert Chandler, Boris Dralyuk, and Irina Mashinski; and *Cardinal Points: International Literary Quarterly* (online).

I have been helped and encouraged in the writing of this book by many friends and colleagues. My special thanks go to Robert Chandler, Boris Dralyuk, Ilya Kutik, Robyn Marsack, Siân Reynolds, Maria Rybakova, Antony Wood; to Masha Karp and the Pushkin Club, London; and to the staff of Columbia University Press, in particular Christine Dunbar and the anonymous peer reviewer who made many generous and helpful comments.

ABBREVIATIONS

Where possible, references are to K. N. Batyushkov, *Essays in Verse and Prose* (Opyty v stikhakh i proze), ed. I. M. Semenko. Moscow: Nauka, 1977—abbreviated as *Essays*. Other references are as follows:

SP   Konstantin Batyushkov, *Selected Prose* (Izbrannaya proza), ed. P. G. Palamarchuk. Moscow: Sovetskaya Rossiya, 1987.

SPP   Konstantin Batyushkov, *Something About the Poet and Poetry* (Nechto o poete i poezii), ed. V. A. Koshelev. Moscow: Sovremennik, 1985.

CP   Konstantin Batyushkov, *Complete Poems* (Polnoe sobranie stikhotvorenii), ed. N. V. Freedman. Moscow/Leningrad: Sovetskii Pisatel', 1964.

Works Konstantin Batyushkov, *Works* (Sochineniya), ed. D. D. Blagoy. Moscow/Leningrad: Academia, 1934.

WP   Vyacheslav Koshelev, *Konstantin Batyushkov: Wanderings and Passions* (Konstantin Batyushkov: stranstviya i strasti). Moscow: Sovremennik, 1987.

WRITINGS FROM THE GOLDEN AGE OF RUSSIAN POETRY

INTRODUCTION

Konstantin Batyushkov (1787–1855) was one of Russia's greatest poets. As such he was celebrated by an even greater poet, Osip Mandelstam, a century later. In 1932, Mandelstam was a literary outcast living in poverty in Moscow, where he wrote a poem addressed to his hero. It was one of the last poems to be published in his lifetime (in the journal *Novy Mir*):

BATYUSHKOV

Like a flâneur with a magic cane,
tender Batyushkov lives at my place—
wanders down Zamostie lanes,
sniffs a rose, sings Zafna's praise.

Not for a moment believing that we
could be separated, I bowed to him:
I shake his brightly gloved cold hand
in an envious delirium.

He smiled at me. "Thank you," I said,
so shy I could not find the words:

No one commands such curves of sound,
never was there such speech of waves.

With oblique words he made us feel
the wealth and torments that we share—
the buzz of verse-making, brotherhood's bell
and the harmonies of pouring tears.

And the mourner of Tasso answered me:
"I am not yet used to eulogy;
I only cooled my tongue by chance
on the grape-flesh of poetry."

All right, raise your eyebrows in surprise,
city dweller and city dweller's friend—
like blood samples, from glass to glass
keep pouring your eternal dreams.[1]

"Tender Batyushkov lives at my place"—Mandelstam had in his room a portrait of the poet, perhaps a very well-known one, where the eyebrows do indeed seem to be raised in surprise. And Batyushkov certainly lived with him—as early as 1910 he had alluded in a poem to an anecdote in which the mentally ill poet, being asked the time, answered, "Eternity." The poem of 1932 shows a great closeness to the subject: "Zafna" is the addressee of Batyushkov's poem "The Torrent"; the marvelous evocation of his "curves of sound" and "speech of waves" recalls the enthusiasm of his contemporaries for the music of Batyushkov's verse; "the mourner of Tasso" refers primarily to the great elegy "Tasso Dying"; and the modesty of the final two stanzas is attested by many descriptions of the poet and by the deprecating way he often wrote of his poetry.

The last two lines present Batyushkov as a predecessor, spilling out poems and dreams like blood and wine (a kind of Eucharist) to keep alive the brotherhood of poets with their "harmonies of pouring tears." In 1932, in the face of exclusion and persecution, the need for such forefathers was pressing; Mandelstam found them not only in Batyushkov, but in the Italian poets that his predecessor had loved, imitated, and translated: Tasso, Ariosto, Petrarch. They offered an example of living lightness—just as Batyushkov is seen as an elegant "flâneur," almost a dandy with his "magic cane," a poet of roses and love, poles apart from the grim literary functionaries who dominated the recently founded Union of Writers of the USSR.

■ □ ■

So who was this "tender Batyushkov" whose image radiated light for the beleaguered Mandelstam? To most non-Russian readers his name is hardly known, but for Russians he is a classic. After the first flowering of Russian poetry in the eighteenth century, characterized above all by the great odes of Lomonosov and Derzhavin, the new poetry of the nineteenth century was largely created by two figures, Batyushkov and the translator and romantic ballad-writer Vasily Zhukovsky. Both were born in the 1780s and lived through the Napoleonic wars; both belonged to Arzamas, the literary grouping out of which emerged in the 1820s the magnificently varied poetry of what was later to be called the Golden Age or the "Pushkin Pléiade." Aleksandr Pushkin regarded Batyushkov as a master.

He did not leave a large volume of poetry, but contemporaries saw in it a practical demonstration of the new heights that the Russian literary language could reach. When in 1821–1823, John Bowring presented Russian poetry to the English-speaking world in his groundbreaking *Specimens of the Russian Poets*, Batyushkov was given a prominent place with a rather good translation of his long-verse epistle, "My Penates." What is more, some lines from the same poem are picked out as an epigraph to the volume, printed daringly in Russian; they celebrate his fellow poets, the priests of the muses.

Many contemporaries gave descriptions of Batyushkov. A close female friend, E. G. Pushkina, left this beautiful, perhaps idealized, portrait:

> Batyushkov was short of stature; he had high shoulders, a hollow chest, red and naturally curly hair, blue eyes and a languid look. A touch of melancholy in all his features combined with his paleness and the softness of his voice to give his whole physiognomy an elusive expression. He had a poetic imagination; there was even more poetry in his soul. He was an enthusiast for everything beautiful. Every virtue seemed accessible to him. Friendship was his idol, selflessness and honesty his essential traits of character. When he was speaking, his features became more animated with movement, and inspiration shone in his eyes. His free, elegant, pure speech gave great charm to his conversation. Carried away by his imagination, he often elaborated sophisms, and if he did not always convince his interlocutors, at least he did not irritate them, since a deeply felt enthusiasm is always excusable in itself and wins the listener's indulgence. I loved his conversation, and even more so his silence. How often I took pleasure in guessing even his fleeting thoughts and the feelings that filled his soul at a time when he seemed plunged in reverie!

> (*WP*, 194–95)

Batyushkov, too, tried to describe himself, insisting rather more on the negative side, his nervous, troubled nature, his tendency to what Baudelaire would soon be calling "spleen." He was a great reader of Montaigne, and like him he attempted to fathom and sum up his own variable and contradictory nature. The result is found in many letters to friends, above all those to his bosom friend, Nikolay Gnedich, translator of Homer, but also, most strikingly, in a self-portrait of 1817, a Romantic Jekyll-and-Hyde image that I should like to quote in full as an introduction to his story. Batyushkov pretends to be writing of a "strange person" he has recently met:

He is about thirty. He is sometimes healthy, very healthy, sometimes ill, at death's door. Today he is as carefree and fickle as a child, but tomorrow you'll find him deep in thought and religion, gloomier than a monk. His face is as good-natured as his heart, but also as changeable. He is thin and dry, and as pale as a sheet. He has lived through three wars; in camp he was full of health, but on leave—a dying man! On the march he was never downcast, always willing to sacrifice his life in a miraculously carefree way which even he was surprised by; in society he finds everything wearisome and the smallest obligation of any kind is a lead weight to him. When duty calls, he does what he has to do selflessly, just as he doses himself with rhubarb when he is ill without batting an eyelid. But what good is there in this? Where does it lead? There are few obligations which he considers a duty, because his little head likes philosophizing— but in such a twisted way that he is constantly suffering from it. He served in the army and in the civil service; very assiduously and very unsuccessfully in the former, in the latter successfully and not at all assiduously. Both types of service he found wearisome, because in reality he is no lover of ranks and medals. Yet he wept when he was passed over and not given a medal. He is as irritable as a dog, and as docile as a sheep.

There are two men in him: one is good-hearted, simple, cheerful, obliging, god-fearing, excessively sincere, generous, sober, agree- able; the other is malevolent, sly, envious, greedy, sometimes (but not often) mercenary, gloomy, grumpy, capricious, discontented, vindictive, crafty, excessively given to pleasure, inconstant in love, and ambitious in every way. This man, the dark one, is a real monster. Both men live in one body. How does this happen? I don't know; I only know that this strange fellow has the profile of a villain, but if you look into his eyes you see a good man: you just have to look carefully and for a long time. This is why I love him! Woe to the person who knows him in profile!

There is more to come. He possesses some talents, yet he has no talent. He has succeeded in nothing, but is always writing. His mind is very capacious, and very narrow. His patience is very limited, whether because of illness or some other cause; his attention is easily distracted, his memory feeble, weakened by reading; just judge for yourself whether he will succeed in anything. In society he is sometimes very agreeable, and sometimes attractive in a special way when people consider his good heart, his carefree mind and his easygoing behavior to others; but when they think of his egoism, self-satisfaction, stubbornness and weariness of soul, everyone sees in him my man in profile. He can be amazingly eloquent; he can make a good entrance and speak well; but he can also be obtuse, tongue-tied and shy. He has lived in hell; he has been on Olympus, as you can see by looking at him. He is blessed and cursed by some spirit. For three days he will think about good deeds and want to perform them—then suddenly his patience will snap and on the fourth day he will be ill-tempered and ungrateful; don't look at his profile then! He is capable of speaking very sharply, and often writes caustically about his neighbor. But the other man, the good one, loves people and weeps bitterly at the epigrams of the dark man. The light man saves the dark one with his tears to the creator, tears of real repentance and good deeds toward humanity. The bad man spoils everything, hinders everything; he is haughtier than Satan, whereas the light man is as good-hearted as a guardian angel. In what strange way can two make one here, how can evil be so mixed up with good and yet so clearly different from it? Where does he come from, this man—or these men, the dark and the light, who make up my acquaintance? But let us continue our description.

He—but which one, the dark or the light?—he or they both love fame. The dark man can love anything, he is even willing to kneel to Christ if people will praise him, such is his vanity; the light one, by contrast, loves fame as Lomonosov loved it, and is amazed at the impudence of the other. The light man has a tender conscience, the other one a forehead of copper. The light one adores his friends and would go to the stake for them; the dark one wouldn't sacrifice a fingernail to friendship, so ardently does he love himself. But when it is a question of friendship, the dark man is excluded; the light one is on guard! In love . . . but let us not complete the description, it would be both repellent and delightful! Everything good you could say about the light man will be taken for himself by the other. To conclude: these two men, or this one man, is currently living in the country and writing his portrait with pen and ink. Let's wish him a hearty appetite, he is going to dinner.

That man is me! Have you guessed as much by now?

(Essays, 424–27)

One might see in this divided soul an expression of Batyushkov's intermediary historical position—between the urbane sociability of Enlightenment Russia and the rebellious Romantic sensibility that is embodied in Pushkin's Evgeny Onegin or in the Pechorin of Lermontov's *Hero of Our Times*. Certainly Russian critics have repeatedly described him as one of the first of the so-called superfluous men, the gifted rebels without a cause who fill the pages of nineteenth-century Russian literature. What he could not know in 1817—in spite of forebodings expressed in letters to friends—was that this split self would a few years later succumb to an incurable mental illness. If the poet saw himself as a split personality, we can equally see his life as split into two more or less equal parts: the thirty-five years before he collapsed (1787–1822), years filled with poetry, friendship, love and war; and the thirty-three years of his illness (1822–1855), years in which he withdrew from society, failed to find a cure, and wrote almost nothing.

■ □ ■

The corpus of Batyushkov's writings is not very extensive, most of the essential pieces apart from the letters being included in the two volumes of his *Essays in Verse and Prose (Opyty v stikhakh i proze)* of 1817.[2] Ever self-critical, he eliminated quite a bit of early or occasional verse from this selection, and would have omitted more from a second edition. He also seems to have destroyed a number of manuscript poems, and of course his illness prevented him from completing many planned works. Even so, he created work in a number of different genres that opened the way for much subsequent Russian literature.

The first full edition of his writings was published in three volumes in 1885–1887. The third volume contains over three hundred letters, mainly to family and friends, to which over fifty have been added subsequently. They are revealing and often brilliant letters, sometimes mixing prose and verse and echoing the poems; not for nothing did Batyushkov declare in 1817: "letters to friends: that is my real genre." His other prose writing consists of essays, usually on literary or moral subjects, and accounts of places visited, notably the pioneering "Strolls Through Moscow" of 1810, and the 1815 "Walk to the Academy of Fine Art," which ushers in Russian art criticism on the model of Diderot's *Salons*.

Turning to his poetry, the first thing to note is that a good deal of it is translation, or at any rate verse inspired by foreign models—French, Italian, German, English, Latin, and Greek. When he was writing, modern Russian poetry was still young; the writers of his generation sought to enrich their culture with themes, forms, and images worked out in prestigious foreign literatures. His great friend Zhukovsky was no doubt the master translator, whose translations overshadow his "original" work, but Batyushkov too was a great reader and borrower. His translations are invariably free, remaking the foreign original in a new form for a different culture. Nor did he distinguish between translated and original poetry; the two belong equally to him and are inextricably mingled in his 1817 volume of verse.

One of his characteristic genres, however, is not translated, though it had foreign models: the verse epistle to friends. He wrote such epistles throughout his career; they range from short passages embedded in actual letters in prose to such long missives as "My Penates," which set the standard for such writing among his immediate successors. The epistles are sprightly, written in rapid short lines, and characteristically moving from mock gravity to much more down-to-earth matters, but also to passages of genuine feeling. There are many other kinds of "light verse," to use Batyushkov's expression—poems of love, friendship, and social life. For him, such verse, as against the solemn ode of the eighteenth-century lyrical tradition, was essential in modern society.

Not all his verse was "light," of course; in particular, the year 1812, with the French invasion and the burning of Moscow, marked a turning point in his view of things. This change figures first in an epistle to his friend Dashkov, which was followed over the years by a number of elegies, serious, sometimes tragic poems of love, friendship, history, poetry, war, and death. The elegy of personal feeling was to be the major genre of Golden Age Russian poetry, and Batyushkov can be seen as its principal creator. Some of his most memorable poems, such as "Shade of a Friend" and "Tasso Dying" are of this kind. But then, toward the end of his creative life, after the publication of the two volumes of 1817, he wrote what many have seen as his masterpieces, the short poems contained in "From the Greek Anthology" and "Imitations of the Ancients."

Batyushkov himself stressed the connection between his life and his poetry. "Write as you live, and live as you write" was his motto. In his letters he is often unduly modest about what he calls his "scribblings." Such is the message of an epistle that he wrote in 1815 and then used as an introduction to the first—and only—selection of his poems published in his lifetime:

TO MY FRIENDS

Here is my book of verse,
Which may perhaps be precious to my friends.
A kindly spirit tells me
That in this maze of words and rhymes
Art is in short supply:
But friends will find my feelings here,
The story of my passions,
Delusions of my mind and heart;
Cares, worries, sorrows of my earlier years,
And light-winged pleasures;
How I would fall, then rise,
Then vanish from the world,
Trusting my little boat to fate.
And, in a word, my friends will find
The diaries of a carefree poet here,
And having found them, say:
"Our friend was often credulous,
Fickle in love, in poetry eccentric,
But he was always true to friendship;

He wearied no one with his poems
    (A wonder on Parnassus!)
    He lived just as he wrote . . .
    Not well, not badly!"

(Essays, 200)

To say that "art is in short supply" is a typically modest disclaimer; in fact, Batyushkov paid great attention to perfecting the language and form of his poetry. Nevertheless, in a letter to Zhukovsky in December 1815, he distinguishes himself from the majority of readers who see poetry as "rhymes, not feelings, words, not images" (*SP*, 387). For the most part his poems are not openly autobiographical, but even apparently impersonal texts are usually an expression of his feelings. In the present book, I shall follow the thread of Batyushkov's writings to explore his troubled life, his passions, delusions, cares, worries, sorrows and light-winged pleasures, setting all these against the changing world of Russian society from Catherine the Great to Nicholas I.

VOLOGDA TO ST. PETERSBURG

Konstantin Nikolaevich Batyushkov was born in Vologda in northern Russia in May 1787 and died there in July 1855. This makes him a near-contemporary of Byron, Stendhal, and the composer Carl Maria von Weber; younger than the English Lake poets; older than Shelley, Leopardi, or Lamartine. As far as Russian poetry is concerned, he belonged to the generation following that of the great poet Gavrila Derzhavin (whom he praised as the "giant of Parnassus")[1] and the fable writer Ivan Krylov. With his friends Vasily Zhukovsky (four years his senior) and Pyotr Vyazemsky (five years his junior), he can be seen as an immediate forerunner of the great flowering of Russian poetry associated with the names of Aleksandr Pushkin, Evgeny Baratynsky, Anton Delvig, Nikolay Yazykov, and many more.

The prime of his life was the time when Russia was at war with the armies of Napoleon, and indeed Batyushkov might well have been a character in *War and Peace*. The first scene in Tolstoy's novel takes place in July 1805 in a St. Petersburg salon such as the eighteen-year-old Konstantin frequented at that time. The world he knew was very much the world of the novel, a society held between the opposite poles of St. Petersburg and Moscow, and between city and country, but for several years turned topsy-turvy by foreign wars and invasion, a society where social success depended largely on family, patronage, and marriage. Like Prince Andrey and Nikolay Rostov, Batyushkov joined the fight against Napoleon, being wounded not at Austerlitz, but at the battle of Heilsberg, just before Friedland and Tilsit. Later he missed the battle of Borodino, but saw the smoking ruins of Moscow (like Pierre Bezukhov), then marched west in pursuit of Napoleon and entered Paris with the Russian army in 1814. In 1820, the date Tolstoy gives to his Epilogue, Batyushkov was coming to the end of his active life and showing signs of mental disturbance, but he lived on until 1855, by which time Tolstoy was approaching the age of thirty and thinking toward his great novel of the Napoleonic wars.

Batyushkov was born during the reign of Catherine the Great and died just after Tsar Nicholas I, but his most active years coincided with the reign of Nicholas's elder brother, Alexander I, with whose army he marched into Paris. He encountered Alexander for the first time in 1813 and seems to have had mixed feelings about him. From the early nineteenth century, however, the young poet looked back with admiration to the greatest of the Romanovs, Peter the Great, who had made Russia, permanently if incompletely and controversially, a European nation with a European culture. Batyushkov was proud to belong to this renewed culture, singing Peter's praises in a number of places. Thus, in a dialogue entitled "An Evening at Kantemir's," his protagonist, Prince Kantemir, the Russian poet and ambassador in Paris in the 1730s, explains to his French interlocutors how his once barbarous nation has been transformed:

> You know what Peter did for Russia; he created people—no! he developed all the spiritual potential in them; he cured them of the disease of ignorance; and the Russians, under the guidance of a great man, proved in a short time that talents *belong to the whole of humanity.*

(Essays, 43)

Peter was not particularly interested in literature, but in creating a modern state. To do this, he needed an educated people, and he created institutions of learning that would transform the cultural life of the elite. And not just the elite: the Academy of Sciences of St. Petersburg, founded in 1724, subsequently the Imperial Academy, gave an education to the commoner Mikhailo Lomonosov, who became a prominent academician and the father of modern Russian literature (the University of Moscow bears his name today). In one of his essays, Batyushkov presents Lomonosov as the Peter the Great of Russian language and literature:

> He achieved as much in the difficult sphere of literature as Peter the Great had in the sphere of politics. Peter the Great awakened a nation sleeping in the fetters of ignorance; he gave it laws, military power and fame. Lomonosov awakened the language of this sleeping people; he gave it eloquence and poetry, he tested its strength in every genre and prepared reliable means to success for future talents.
>
> (*Essays, 9*)

Batyushkov and his friends were to be counted among these "future talents."

If Russian literature was to take its place in the concert of European literatures, it had to learn from foreign examples, just as Peter had served his apprenticeship in the shipyards of Holland, bringing back to Russia foreign craftsmen and specialists of all kinds. Naturally, therefore, translation played a central role in the creation of Russian literary culture in the eighteenth and early nineteenth centuries. German writers and scientists were influential, but the dominant model was France. Paris was the cultural capital of Europe, French increasingly became the second language of educated Russians, and the Russian nobility began to travel to France. Kantemir, as we have seen, was at home in Paris in the 1730s; his satires are written in French-style syllabic verse, and were published in London in French translation. He was aiming to be the Russian Boileau, and many of his successors were seen as the Russian Racine, Molière, Voltaire, or La Fontaine.

By the second half of the eighteenth century, the enlightenment culture of France was epitomized in the figure of Voltaire, with his readable witty critique of existing abuses, superstition, and obscurantism; Voltaire and the *philosophes* were eagerly read in the new Russia by Batyushkov, among others. But France also offered models of salon poetry; by the end of the century, French poetry tended to mean above all light, *galant* verse—witty, erotic, and sentimental. Among the young Batyushkov's models we find representatives of successive generations, Jean-Baptiste Gresset (1709–1777), Évariste de Parny (1753–1814), and Charles-Hubert Millevoye (1782–1816). All of these are largely forgotten today, but Parny in particular had a great reputation among the young Russian poets of the early nineteenth century. In one of her poems, Anna Akhmatova has the schoolboy Pushkin strolling outside his school, in the park of Tsarskoe Selo, with a "dog-eared copy of Parny."[2]

Of course, by the time Pushkin was at school around 1812, France was not primarily the place of enlightenment and light verse. In the first place, it had become the land of revolution, to which the Russians, like other European peoples, reacted variously, ranging from enthusiasm to horror. Revolution was followed by foreign conquests under Napoleon; in Batyushkov's eyes, as we shall see, the invasion of the Napoleonic armies and the destruction of Moscow meant that French enlightenment had given way to barbarism. In Russian literature more generally, the new century brought a change of models, with French enlightened classicism giving way to the romanticism of Northern Europe, which was made available to Russians by some major translations. In the first decade of the nineteenth century, Vasily Zhukovsky helped create a new poetry with his versions of Gray's "Elegy" and German ballads. Even before this came the vogue for an imagined ancient Celtic culture generated by James Macpherson's "translations" of Ossian. Kostrov's complete Russian Ossian was published in 1792, and several of Batyushkov's poems show him succumbing to the charm of the northern bard.

■ □ ■

Vologda, where Batyushkov was born and died, is an ancient city of northern Russia. Situated some 200 miles to the north of Moscow, and some 250 miles to the east of St. Petersburg, it occupied a strategic position on the trading routes connecting Novgorod, Moscow, and Archangel. As a child, Batyushkov lived for several years on his grandfather's estate at Danilovskoe, southwest of Vologda, and he later inherited from his mother the estate of Khantonovo, between Vologda and Novgorod. Between the ages of twenty and thirty-five, Batyushkov led a wandering life; his destiny carried him from place to place, both within Russia and abroad, to Germany, Finland, France, England, Sweden, Italy. In these years, Khantonovo was the country base to which straitened circumstances and inclination frequently forced him to return, and where he had the leisure to write.

In one of his essays, Batyushkov speaks of the formative influence of the places where poets spend their earliest years. Following Montesquieu's theories about the dependence of culture on climate, he writes:

> The climate, the sight of sky, water and earth, all this works on the poet's impressionable soul. We see in the songs of the Scandinavian scalds and the Erse bards something severe, dark, wild and invariably meditative, reminding us of the overcast northern sky, the sea

mists, and a nature poor in the gifts of life but always majestic and delightful, even in its horror.

(Essays, 26–27)

Batyushkov is thinking here of the poems attributed to Ossian, which swept through literary Russia in his youth, but he finds this northern character too in the writing of his hero Lomonosov, who came from Arkhanglesk in the far north:

> I see in my mind's eye how, full of inspiration,
> A youth stands silently above the raging ocean,
> His mind alive with dreams and sweet new thoughts,
> Hearing the waves' monotonous uproar.

("Epistle to I. M. Muravyov-Apostol," Essays, 283)

Derzhavin, Batyushkov's great predecessor, is imagined similarly, haunted by the sights and sounds of his Volga childhood.

It is not surprising then if he presents himself as a "Hyperborean," a child of the North. In "The Traveler and the Stay-at-Home," a long fable about the dangers and the charms of travel, he has his exhausted traveler returning to Athens only to set off again in search of a land of eternal spring, to find roses in "the snows of the Hyperboreans" (*Essays*, 319). Batyushkov himself, responsive as he was to the charms of the Bay of Naples during his diplomatic service there, still found himself longing for home. Home might mean Moscow or St. Petersburg, but also the run-down estate at Khantonovo, a wooden mansion set on a hill looking over the grandiose Sheksna River and the immense forests and marshes of the North. Not that he was always happy there, far from it. Like Pushkin's Evgeny Onegin, he found boredom lying in wait for him in the country, where he lived a lonely life. In a letter of November 1809 to his best friend, Nikolay Gnedich, he writes: "Time passes quickly, then slowly, there is more bad than good, more stupidity than intelligence . . . In my house all is quiet; the dog is dozing at my feet, looking at the fire in the stove, my sister is in another room, reading old letters, I think . . . I have picked up a book again and again, and it has fallen from my hands" (*SP*, 286). In the winter it could be fearfully cold too, prompting the poet to a flash of doggerel in a letter to his friend:

> I'm shivering with cold,
> Though I'm sitting by the stove,
> Lying under my coat
> I see the fire's glow,
> But I tremble like a vole,
> Or like a wretched mole,
> I love the warmth of coal
> But I wander through the cold,
> Only verse keeps me whole.
>
> (*CP, 248*)

But if Khantonovo sometimes seemed like a desert, it could also bloom, as when the poet created for himself a poetic summerhouse in the garden, writing to Gnedich in May 1817: "For the first time in my life I have arranged a summerhouse to my taste in the garden. It cheers me up so much that I can't leave my writing desk" (*SPP*, 325). And in a poem of the same time, "The Muses' Arbor," he writes of the acacia and the bird-cherry, the flowers and the bees that surrounded him here, even among the dark forests of the North.

Batyushkov was ambivalent about his country home, then— as he was to be ambivalent about the cities where he lived, his native Vologda, the capital St. Petersburg where he studied and worked, Moscow where he had good friends, Paris into which he marched with the Allied armies, Naples where he served as a diplomat. He lived a nomadic life, not really belonging anywhere, but the North was where he began and ended, and in poem after poem he speaks warmly and reverently of his "Lares and Penates," the household gods.

■ □ ■

Batyushkov was born into an old gentry family. There are records of his ancestors from the sixteenth century. One of them, Ivan Mikhailovich, is mentioned as an officer in Ivan the Terrible's campaign against Kazan. By the seventeenth century, the family had acquired a good deal of property in the Vologda region, but this wealth ebbed away so that Batyushkov, although a serf-owning landowner, was always short of money. His paternal grandfather Lev Andreevich was a notable public figure and managed his estate efficiently; he had a great influence on young Konstantin, who spent several years of his childhood in the old-world country house at Danilovskoe. By all accounts, Lev Andreevich was at this time a vigorous, strong-minded old man.

The father, Nikolay L'vovich, cuts a somewhat less impressive figure, though he was a well-read man with a fine library, and was keen for his son to receive the best possible education. In his youth he was almost caught up in the supposedly seditious doings of his mentally disturbed uncle Ilya (who incurred the wrath of Catherine the Great). Nikolay himself, after a brief period of disgrace, served for a time in the army; by the time of his son's birth he was an officer of the law (*prokuror*) in Vologda. Some time in the 1780s he had married Aleksandra Grigor'evna Berdyaeva, who bore him five children—Konstantin's three older sisters (Anna, Elizaveta, and Aleksandra), Konstantin, and his younger sister Varvara. Aleksandra never married and devoted herself to her brother's welfare when he fell ill. Of the poet's mother we know very little, except that she died in 1795, when he was only seven. She is largely absent from his writings, and we can only guess at the effect of her early loss. Her death was attributed to the "derangement of her mental faculties"—an ominous anticipation of what would befall her son. Her quite considerable estate (including Khantonovo) passed to Konstantin and his sisters when they came of age, but this was not enough to protect him from a recurrent shortage of funds.

We have little direct evidence of Batyushkov's early years, and he himself wrote very little about them. In spite of the positive influence of his Danilovskoe grandfather, he probably had a rather disturbed childhood. Unlike most children of the gentry, he seems not to have had any home-based tutors (the "Monsieur" and "Madame" that Pushkin writes of in *Eugene Onegin*). But in 1797, after his mother's death, he was sent to a boarding school in St. Petersburg, a *pension* run by a French teacher. Batyushkov was thus exposed early on to the hegemonic French culture, and it is no surprise that he translated and imitated several French poets. More interesting for his later life and writings is the fact that after three or four years he moved to a school run by an Italian. Here he began to acquire an unusual fluency in Italian; in later years, even before his diplomatic service in Italy between 1818 and 1821, Italian literature was to be particularly important to him.

At various times he translated or imitated Boccaccio, Petrarch, Ariosto, Tasso, and the satirist Giovanni Battista Casti. As a young man, he planned to make a complete translation of Tasso's epic *Jerusalem Delivered* (La Gerusalemme liberata); only fragments were completed, but he wrote a long poem on the death of Tasso—with whose tragic fate he identified. And his prose works include essays on Petrarch, Ariosto, and Tasso. The beginning of the essay on Ariosto and Tasso explains something of their charms, especially for a reader in a northern country. He gives pride of place to the sonorous beauty of the language, a feature that he attempted to imitate in Russian poetry:

There is a special charm attached to learning the Italian language. This supple, sonorous, delightful language, nurtured beneath the fortunate skies of Rome, Naples and Sicily, amid political upheavals and then at the brilliant Medici court, a language given shape by great writers, by the best poets, by learned men and profound statesmen—this language has become capable of expressing all sights and all forms. It possesses a character different from other modern idioms and vernacular languages, all of which show signs of harshness, confused and savage sounds, slowness of speech and something characteristic of the North.

(Essays, 138)

Batyushkov was thus unusually well endowed with foreign languages for a young man of his generation, and was correspondingly well read in literature, philosophy, and history. In addition to French and Italian, he knew some German (he translated scenes of Schiller's *The Bride of Messina* [Die Braut von Messina]) and possibly a little English—and as we have seen he was open to the winds blowing from the North, whether it be Byron, Ossian, or the scalds of old Scandinavia. But as has so often been the case, Italy, the Mediterranean, and the ancient world of Greece and Rome were particularly appealing to a man from Northern Europe. The lost world of the classics haunted him, as it haunted such different figures as Goethe, Hölderlin, Shelley, and Batyushkov's younger compatriot Evgeny Baratynsky. He did not know the ancient languages as well as the modern ones. When he translated poems from the Greek Anthology, he worked from French versions provided by a Russian friend. As for Latin, although he used epigraphs from the Roman poets and translated enough of Tibullus to be called "the Russian Tibullus," he still needed to eke out his own Latin by using French translations. But whatever his linguistic competence, the poets of Greece and Rome, from

Anacreon and Sappho to Horace and Propertius, were close to his heart, as was the culture they spoke for. One of Batyushkov's most affecting poems is a beautifully composed short piece written in 1819 after visiting the ruins of a famous Roman resort, the baths of Baiae in the Bay of Naples.

Such mastery came later in Batyushkov's life. Already at school, though, he was writing poetry. Almost all of it has vanished, but it is interesting to look at the first of his poems to have survived, "Dreaming." Written in 1802–1803, when the poet was fifteen, it was sufficiently important in his eyes to be rewritten several times; the original 89 lines were expanded to 211 by the time it was published in the 1817 edition of his works. Pushkin—who admired Batyushkov greatly—did not think much of it, even in its revised form, annotating it with remarks such as "childish verse," "crude," and "the weakest of all his poems."[3] In its original form it is certainly derivative, owing a lot to Batyushkov's uncle, the poet Mikhail Muravyov, but also to Western Romanticism and notably to the *Poems of Ossian*. At the same time, it announces a constant theme, the dissatisfaction with reality and the need for "dreaming," by which we should understand imagination. These are the first ten lines:

> O sweetest dreaming, daughter of quiet night,
> Come down in misty clouds from heaven to me,
> Or in the dear face of my fearful love,
> Whose burning eyes are glittering with tears!
>> You who like a ray of light
>> Pierce the tender poet's night,
> You burn like dawn fire and exalt his verses,
> Your favorite, a favorite of the muses,
>> And his grief to him is sweet,
>> For in his grief he dreams.

(CP, 55)

From early on, then, young Konstantin was hooked on poetry. At
the age of sixteen or seventeen, he wrote an "Epistle to My Poems,"
which ends:

> Long, long ago it became clear to me
> That I'd have lived my life out quietly
> If wretched Phoebus hadn't made me crazy;
> I would disdain the thrills of being famous,
> And happy as a pasha in Kashmir
> I'd never dream of muses, poems or lyre.
> But no ... my poems, I can't live without you;
> Your rhymes and meters are my second nature!
> It's my misfortune, my infirmity—
> Poems, like women, are a necessity;
> If they don't love us, we should really scorn them,
> But they are beautiful, and we adore them.

(CP, 58–59)

The young author of these lines had left school a couple of years
earlier. His formal schooling was short, but the gaps in his educa-
tion were to be amply filled by his time in St. Petersburg society,
where his good fortune allowed him to spend the years from 1802
to 1806 under the care, and in the house, of his kinsman Mikhail
Muravyov.

Muravyov, born in 1757, belonged to the same generation as
Batyushkov's father and had served as tutor to the future tsar, Alex-
ander I; he then became a senator and an important figure in the
ministry of education, where he found a not too demanding job for
his young nephew, who was never to feel at home in the tedium of
government service. Muravyov was a man of great learning, and it
was to him that the young poet owed his knowledge and love of

the Latin and Greek classics. More generally, he seems to have been an influential father figure, passing on to Batyushkov some of his values, his moral sense, his taste for domestic and family life, his cult of friendship, his love of studious retirement (the Lares and Penates that figure so much in the younger man's poems). Muravyov was also a significant poet, a member of the "sentimentalist" school grouped around Karamzin.[4] In his verse, the expression and exploration of private feelings tends to replace the more public concerns of the eighteenth-century ode. At the same time, the formal language and structure of the ode give way to the more conversational form of the epistle, the verse letter to friends, and also to various forms of light verse—on the model of French *poésies légères*. In all these matters, Batyushkov followed closely in the footsteps of his uncle and later wrote an essay in homage to him.

If St. Petersburg life meant earnest conversations with the uncle, it also meant the "salon" of the aunt—one of the first Russian salons. Here the young man encountered the charms of women—married women and young girls—and here he learned to love and flirt and play. As he later put it in a letter, ". . . I loved, crowned with lily of the valley, in a pink tunic with a staff and green ribbons—green, the color of hope—innocent at heart, with eyes full of feeling, and singing little ditties: 'Who could with such passion love' or 'I am content, yet malcontent' or 'Nowhere I can find a place' " (*WP*, 39). All very innocent then, or so it seems, it allowed Batyushkov to make a name for himself as a poet of love and pleasure, an Epicurean poet. This is the figure he cuts in one of his earliest poems, originally entitled "Advice to Friends" in 1805 and later extensively rewritten to be called "The Joyful Hour." Here is the first version, in which the poetry of love, wine, and roses slides naturally into the theme of death—as in Poussin's painting, *Et in Arcadia ego*, where classical shepherds cluster around a tomb.

With his "oaten flute," or reed pipe, Batyushkov plays the shepherd
of pastoral poetry:

ADVICE TO FRIENDS

Faut-il être tant volage,
Ai-je dit au doux plaisir...

(Henriette de Murat)[5]

Give me a simple oaten flute,
My friends, and all sit down around me,
Where coolness lingers through the heat
In the thick shadows of the elm tree;
Come close, sit down and lend an ear
To the wise guidance of my muses:
In the short days of the young year
If happiness is what you're seeking,
Dear friends, abandon fame, that specter,
Play pleasure's games while you're still young,
And as you dance through life's path, scatter
Roses; and flourish, lovely youth!
Watered by a pure spring, flourish,
If only for a few short days,
Like a rose, shaded by myrtle,
Among the laughing fields of May!
Let us taste the joys of living,
Find flowers growing on the thorns!
Time flies; there isn't long for playing,
Not long for glorying in life's charms.
Not long—but time to forget sadness,
To drown in a sweet dream of gladness:

Dreams are the source of happiness!
Ah! must we always mope and sigh
Without a smile for lovely May?
Better far to take our ease
And with a beautiful young girl
Go dancing beneath the shady trees,
Then, winding an arm around her waist
And breathing love, nothing but love,
Quietly, quietly, we shall sigh
And press a heart against a heart.

What bliss! And here is cheerful Bacchus
Pouring his thick, heady wine,
Here in a fine white dress Erata
Sings in our ears a tender tune.
You hasty hours, stay still, give us
Just one more glimpse of happiness!

But no, the happy days race by,
Race by, or like an arrow fly;
No lingering, no heart's delight
Can halt the days' impetuous flight,
And time's strong hand will still destroy
Our calm, our comfort, and our joy!

You cheerful, greenly gleaming meadows,
Clear-watered streams, beloved gardens!
You willows, oaks and aspen glades,
Shall I no more beneath your boughs
Enjoy the freshness of the shade?
Shall I too in a quiet field soon
Lie down to sleep beneath a stone,

My lyre and simple oaten flute
Lying above me on the tomb?
Grass will grow thickly over them,
Grow thickly, and no friendly tears
Will ever water my cold dust!
And should I feel despair at this?
When I die, everything is dead!
But in their somber hands the fates
Keep spinning, spinning my life's thread . . .
Corinna and my friends are here—
Why should I now give way to grief?

If our life runs quickly from us,
If joy itself is not eternal,
Better to live by play and pleasure,
Mingling merriment with wisdom,
Than to pursue fame's empty lure
And yawn with boredom and dull care.

(CP, 74–76)

In the first few years of his poetic career, Batyushkov was to return to these themes again and again. It was as an Epicurean poet that he influenced younger contemporaries.

The young poet flourished in the Muravyov household and met a number of important people there, including the father figure among poets, Gavrila Derzhavin. Even more significant as a meeting place for writers was the circle that gathered in the open house of Muravyov's distant relative Aleksey Nikolaevich Olenin (1763–1843). A little younger than Muravyov, Olenin was still old enough to be Batyushkov's father; he was for Konstantin both a protector and a friend. He was not himself a poet, but a rich nobleman, a powerful public figure interested in all the arts. His salon was active in promoting the fusion of neoclassicism and sentimentalism that lies behind much of Batyushkov's writing. Olenin's principal interests were the plastic arts and archaeology, and it was in this area that he influenced theatrical practice, advising the star playwright of the period, Vladislav Ozerov, on the designs for his historical plays such as *Oedipus at Athens* and *Fingal*. The second of these tragedies was based on the poems of Ossian, whom we have already come across among Batyushkov's enthusiasms.[6]

Batyushkov admired Ozerov's work and sympathized with him. Indeed, he went so far as to write a fable, "The Shepherd and the Nightingale" (much appreciated by the playwright), in an attempt to console and encourage Ozerov after critics of the opposing camp (conservative defenders of traditional classicism) had attacked and satirized his patriotic tragedy *Dmitry Donskoy*. Later he was to compare Ozerov with his hero Torquato Tasso, seeing both of them as driven to despair and madness by hostile criticism.

Batyushkov rubbed shoulders with many other significant writers in Olenin's circle. There was Derzhavin, of course, but also the fable writer Ivan Krylov, for whom Batyushkov expressed unwavering admiration, the great historian Nikolay Karamzin, and established poetic luminaries such as Vasily Kapnist and Ippolit Bogdanovich. But his great friend was Nikolay Gnedich, three years his senior, a young poet from what is now Ukraine. He had grown up in a poor family, but unlike Batyushkov, he studied at Moscow University before moving to St. Petersburg, where he became Batyushkov's colleague in the ministry of education. The two friends were very different in appearance and character: Batyushkov small, mobile, and impressionable; Gnedich tall, one-eyed (as a result of a childhood bout of smallpox), serious, and self-reliant. They complemented one another, with Gnedich taking on the role of tutor and protector to his younger friend and eventually seeing to the publication of his works. Some time around 1806, they agreed each to translate a major epic poem, the *Iliad* for Gnedich, Tasso's *Jerusalem Delivered* (La Gerusalemme liberata) for Batyushkov. Gnedich carried his task through to the end, creating the standard Russian Homer, whereas Batyushkov managed to complete only a small fragment of Tasso's poem.

In 1811–1812, Batyushkov composed a poem celebrating the type of classic male friendship to which he aspired:

FRIENDSHIP

> Happy the man who has found a bosom friend,
> The man who loves and is loved by a sensitive soul!
> Even on Cocytus' banks Theseus does not suffer,
> For he has with him his soul-mate Pirithous.
> Orestes lies in chains—but we only envy him:
> Pylades his friend is with him . . . under the blade.
> And you, youthful Achilles, greathearted warrior,
> Immortal paragon of heroes and friends,
> Your greatness lies in friendship; this was your life,
> And having avenged your friend with a fearless hand,
> Happy! you fell dead on the funeral pyre.

(Essays, 221)

In literature, if not in war, he found a friendship of this kind with Gnedich. It finds expression in a fascinating and moving series of letters between the two men; writing to Gnedich, Batyushkov is at his most mercurial, a free spirit, witty and irreverent. Something of this comes across in the verse epistles that he wrote to his friend, sometimes enclosing them in prose letters. One of the earliest of these, written in 1806, echoes the Epicurean sentiments of "Advice to Friends," and is written in the short lines that were Batyushkov's favorite form for his epistles to friends. The particular question

raised here is that of literary fame, which was a constant preoc-
cupation, as he admitted in the double self-portrait quoted in the
introduction. The author of these disenchanted lines was a mere
eighteen years old:

TO GNEDICH

Only friendship offers me
Immortality's proud wreath,
But it is wilting visibly
Like a daisy in the heat.
Can fame tempt me from the road
Of pleasure, a road so modest?
Pleasure's pathway is well-trodden;
The road to fame is steep and hard.
Should I chase an empty specter
And gather laurels wearily?
I who know the arts of pleasure
Like a child who loves to play
And am happy . . . Thus far flowers
Strewed the path to happiness;
Singing, dreaming, or consoling
My sad heart by weaving verse,
I would sing in idle leisure
And the muse was my dear friend,
Not my sovereign. But at present
My spring is coming to an end,
Fading like a light-winged vision,
Dragging with it as it goes
Charms of dreaming and of singing!
Tender myrtles, tender flowers,
Which the lovely girls once plaited

For the poet's head, are faded!
Ah! can fame be compensation
For the loss of happiness?
Can its coming bring salvation
As my sun begins to set?

(*CP, 76–77*)

Unlike Gnedich, who persevered with his task, Batyushkov was nagged by self-doubt and shifted from one thing to another, while still clinging to the desire to be a great poet.

The early years of the nineteenth century saw a flourishing of literary societies in the Russian cities, groupings of mainly young male writers united by the idealistic love of poetry, ideas, and civilized values and the ambition of creating a new Russian literature. One of the earliest of these was the Free Society of Lovers of Literature, Science and the Arts, founded in St. Petersburg in 1801. This gathered together a variety of young men, including several of Batyushkov's colleagues at the ministry of education. With official permission the Society published journals and other collective works. Batyushkov, barely eighteen, was admitted as a member in 1805, his earliest offering being an adaptation to contemporary Russian society of Boileau's first satire. He was to return to satire frequently, sometimes a general mockery of pride, philistinism, and other social vices, but more often a contribution to the literary polemics of the age, the Russian quarrel of Ancients and Moderns, where Batyushkov and his allies did battle with the archaizing conservatism of the group centered on Admiral Shishkov. As we shall see in later chapters, his sharp pen did good service—not for nothing was he given the nickname "Achilles."

Batyushkov didn't remain deeply involved with the Free Society for long. Indeed, soon after he joined it, its charismatic president, the poet Ivan Pnin, died of consumption, and the Society declined. This loss provided the impetus for Batyushkov's first poem in a genre that he later illustrated on several occasions, the elegy of mourning. It is a poem of friendship, "sentimentalist" in its advocacy of humanitarian values (notice the epigraph from Voltaire's poem on the death of the actress Adrienne Lecouvreur). The tone combines the conventional loftiness of a memorial with the quietness of simple feeling; as in many of his later poems of this kind, Batyushkov weaves interesting patterns, using lines of varying length and irregular groupings of rhymes, with an alternation of masculine and feminine endings:

ON THE DEATH OF PNIN

Que vois-je, c'en est fait, je t'embrasse et tu meurs[7]

Voltaire

Where is our friend, our singer? Where are the charms of youth?
Alas, it is all gone, mowed down by death's sharp scythe.
The lyre of the sweet muses' favorite lies abandoned,
He sings no more, like us he was a passing shadow.

Our friend is gone, we seek for him in vain.
    He graced the world for one brief morning.
    He faded like a flower in May
And parted from his friends at life's first dawning.

Pnin lived only for friendship, full of ardent feeling.
Not gold alone he lavished on unhappy men . . .
For what is gold alone? Better shed tears with them.
Pnin strove to help the people of his nation,
His pen defended innocence from destiny.
    Courteous in friendly conversation,
    He made his friends his family.

And now, my friends, as round his grave we gather,

His frigid dust alone is ours.

Now we repeat in grief and tears:

Rest here in peace, dear friend and brother,

Live in our hearts, beloved follower of the muse.

When for the last time we embraced his body,

It seemed the world shared in our grief

Amor himself in sorrow

Put out the light of life.

He did not lay upon his tomb

Sad cypress branches, but a rose in bloom.

(CP, 73–74)

With his farewell to Pnin at the end of 1805, it is as if Batyushkov is anticipating his farewell to the peaceful, protected life he had enjoyed with the Muravyovs. From the end of the following year, he would be caught up in a life of war and travel.

WAR AND PEACE

*What a life I have led for poetry! Three wars, all the time on horseback
and on the highways of the world.*

▸ Letter from Batyushkov to Zhukovsky, June 1817

While young Batyushkov was finding his way in the polite society of St. Petersburg, flirting with women, and taking his first steps as a poet of Epicurean enjoyment, storms were gathering in the west. The First Consul Bonaparte had crowned himself as the Emperor Napoleon in 1804, and after the short-lived peace of Amiens, hostilities between France and the rest of Europe began again. In 1805, as we learn from the first sentence of *War and Peace*, Napoleon annexed Genoa and Lucca; he then turned his attention to the Central Powers, defeating Austria and Prussia in a series of major battles. Russia, under Alexander I, occupied an ambiguous position. Russian forces were on the losing side at Austerlitz and Friedland, but in 1807 Alexander and Napoleon met at Tilsit and signed peace treaties, which among other things opened the way for Russian forces to conquer Finland in the campaign of 1808–1809. Relations between France and Russia soon deteriorated, and Napoleon made the enormous mistake of marching east. He reached Moscow after the bloody but inconclusive battle of Borodino, only to be forced to retreat from the burning city and make his disastrous return to France, harassed by Russian forces. Alexander and his army entered Paris as conquerors in March 1814.

But at the end of 1806, after a series of defeats, Russia's western frontiers were under threat. Indeed, the danger was sufficiently great for the government to call for volunteers. The nineteen-year-old Batyushkov was one of those who responded; in January 1807, he was transferred at his own request from his uninspiring civilian post to a position in the militia, and soon he was marching to meet the enemy in Prussia. His father had not consented to this, and Konstantin had to make his excuses: "I beg your forgiveness for taking this honorable step without your permission or your blessing. . . . I have done this of my own volition and I hope (if I am worthy of it) that our sovereign will reward you generously for your sadness and grief" (*SP*, 279–80).

So why did he take this "honorable step"? Partly, as this letter suggests, in the unrealistic hope of improved career prospects. But as with Tolstoy's young heroes, there were more idealistic motives. The excitement of a military life had glamour for a man who later spoke repeatedly of the boredom he felt in day-to-day life; as we saw above, he wrote of himself: "On the march he was never downcast, always willing to sacrifice his life in a miraculously carefree way; . . . in society he finds everything wearisome." He wanted glory, and no doubt shared with many Russians a genuine upsurge of patriotism.

Batyushkov's attitude to this Russian patriotism is interesting, the more so since he owed so much to French culture. We remember how at the beginning of *War and Peace* the Francophile and largely Francophone members of the St. Petersburg elite unite in condemnation of the French emperor (the exception being Pierre, for whom Napoleon is still the embodiment of revolutionary values). In 1810, Batyushkov was to skewer this contradiction (which he himself shared) in a neat little epigram:

THE TRUE PATRIOT

"O Russian bread and salt![1] O ancestors!
You heirlooms, sweet and simple,
Grandfather's granite will and granny's wimple!
You are our sole recourse!
And yet, and yet, you are forgotten!"
So, at a table spread with bottles,
Firs, sitting with my guests, was holding forth
In words of fire, a Russian champion,
Eating *ragoût*, truffles and *champignons*,
Then he knocked back a magnum of champagne
And then—sat down to play *boston* again.

(Essays, 364–65)

The same sort of fiercely ironic observation is made by Count Rostopchin in book 8 of *War and Peace*.

Whatever his motivations, the poet marched off to war. He remembered this departure ten years later, in an essay in memory of his soldier friend, the even younger Ivan Petin, who died a heroic death at the battle of Leipzig in 1813:

In 1807 we both left the capital and set off on the campaign. I believe in sympathy, because experience has taught me to believe in the inexplicable mysteries of the heart. Our souls were alike. The same passions, the same predilections, the same impetuous and carefree nature that was characteristic of me in my early youth captivated me in my comrade. The habit of being together, enduring together the labors and cares of war, sharing dangers and pleasures, all this bound us more closely.

(Essays, 399)

Batyushkov was full of enthusiasm, and felt happy riding through the fields reading Tasso. Unlike Petin, though, he was not a born soldier. In the self-portrait quoted above we read: "He served in the army and in the civil service, very assiduously and very unsuccessfully in the former." A snatch of verse in a letter sent to Gnedich at the beginning of March sounds a comic note of nostalgia:

Am I condemned to hear just drums of war?
Let friendship's lovely voice amid the clashes
For one short hour restore me to Parnassus
When I have strayed into the ranks of Mars
     And on a doughty Rosinante[2]
     Set off for glory at a canter.

(CP, 241)

A few days later, from Riga, again in a letter to Gnedich, Batyushkov gives a fuller, but by no means heroic, picture of poet as soldier:

Believe me, it's not easy from a sleigh or saddle
With people shouting "Quick March!" or "Eyes right!"
     To write, dear friend, a verse epistle . . .
No—shunning me, the Muses have taken flight
And in St. Petersburg or God knows where
     Hidden their lovely features.
     Without them I am speechless!
If you become a wolf you can't so soon unlearn
The wolfish way of walking and the howl.

So, when a sacred thought arises in my soul
       Not hearing drums that beat,
Or the sharp shouts of stately musketeers,
I urge my poor winged horse to take its flight
Up to Parnassus—or, put otherwise,
       Eschewing eloquence,
A dismal sight rises before my eyes.
The wind from all sides blows through the smashed panes;
A gloomy tomcat woos his feline lover
       And the poor Finn's knapsack
       Falls from his weary back;
The wretch squats in the fireside corner
And with a torn sleeve wipes the tears that linger . . .
Poor children of a climate cold and raw,
Acquainted with hunger, Russian soldiers, war!

(CP, 77–78)

Before long, though, the game turned serious. The Russian army crossed the Prussian frontier and on May 28 and 29 engaged the enemy in the battle of Heilsberg. Batyushkov fought bravely here, and had to be carried off the field half-dead. He gave his version of events in a poem of 1809:

REMEMBERING

Dreams! You have been beside me everywhere,
Strewing the dark road of my life with flowers!
How sweetly in the Heilsberg fields I dreamed
       While the whole camp lay deep in sleep,
And leaning on his spear of steel, the warrior
Gazed into misty distance! In the sky
       The full moon shone, shedding its light

Between the branches on my little hut;
The Alle gently rolled its glowing stream,
Reflecting in its waves the camp and trees.
In the dim hours of night the fires burned low
Beside the sleeping soldier's huts. O fields
      Of Heilsberg! O you lofty hills,
Where I so often in the moonlit night
Sat deep in thought, dreamed of my motherland.
O fields of Heilsberg! Then I did not know
That soldiers' bodies soon would strew your grass,
That from these hills the metal jaws would thunder,
      And I, your happy dreamer, flying
      To meet my death against the foe,
      Would press my hand on a deep wound,
Nearly succumbing at my dawn of life . . . —
The storms of life passed over like a dream! —
      Only dark memory survives . . .
A frontier lies between the past and us;
      Only in dream can we come near it.
And in my memory I now bring back
      To life the terrifying moment
      When in a paroxysm of pain,
      Seeing a hundred deaths before me,
I feared to die far from my native place.
But heaven heard my heartfelt prayers and looked
      With pity on me in my need;
I crossed the Neman, saw the promised land
      And wept and kissed the earth and said:
"Thrice blessed is the man who lives at home
Among his household gods, enjoying the peace,
And never takes a step outside his hut
      And does not with his prayers

Trouble winged Victory!
    He is not blinded by the love of fame
        To sacrifice his peace, his blood:
    He sees his grave and quietly waits for death."

(Essays, 210–11)

The poem, written in the flowing manner characteristic of Batyush-kov's elegies, moves with little warning from the soldier's dreams to the horrors of action; above all, it dramatizes the pull between the glamour of war and the joys of home life (the "household gods") that will recur in his writing.

Batyushkov's injury was indeed serious and was to plague him in later life. In 1808, his bravery at Heilsberg would be rewarded with the Order of St. Anne (third class). Meanwhile he was transferred to Riga to convalesce; another letter to Gnedich tells the tale:

> Dear friend! I am alive. How—God only knows. I was shot right through the leg by a bullet that hit the upper part of my thigh and my behind. The wound is quite deep, but not dangerous, since the bone has apparently not been hit—how this happened I don't know. I am in Riga. I can't convey to you what I had to suffer lying in the cart that brought me here. Our battalion had heavy losses. All the officers are wounded, one dead. The infantry were very brave, crazily so. Who could have imagined all this?

(SP, 281)

Riga turned out to be a place of happiness for the wounded poet. In the two months he spent there, he convalesced in the welcoming house of a local merchant. The poem I have translated as "Remembering" was originally called "Memories of 1807" and had a long concluding section (omitted from the publication of his works in 1817) expressing the poet's gratitude to the "peaceable family" and the "hospitable roof" of his Riga hosts. Above all, Batyushkov remembered the daughter of the house, whom he called Emilia—whether this was her real name or a poetic label remains unclear. Here are some nostalgic lines from what seems to be one of Batyushkov's first genuine love poems:

> Alas, it all has vanished like a sweet dream!
> Where have they gone, the raptures and the kisses,
> And where are you, clandestine nighttime meetings,
> When I would hold her tight in my embrace
> And did not envy even the gods their fate! . . .
>   Now, separated from her,
> I count the weary days, dragging my bitter chain,
> And only memories give me the power
>   To fly to her again
>   And dimly in the night I feel
>   Through dreaming's deep enchantment
> A gentle breeze that bears the fragrance
>   Of flowers, and I breathe
>   Emilia's sweet breath.

(Essays, 535–36)

It is hard to know how much reality there is in the various love poems that Batyushkov left. Sometimes it is clear that he is imitating the erotic or sentimental writings of a Tibullus or a Parny, as in his youthful verses addressed to "Malvina," "Chloe," and others. He describes himself in an epistle to Petin as "equally unhappy in love and war"—and certainly he seems far removed from such enterprising ladies' men as Byron or Pushkin. He may have had passing affairs, but the only woman for whom his love was clearly expressed was Anna Furman, and as we shall see, this love was to remain unrequited. Nevertheless, the tender sentiments expressed in various poems of 1809–1810, even when the poems are in part translations from the French or the Italian, suggest a strong attachment to the memory of the Riga merchant's daughter. Not that it matters greatly to the twenty-first-century reader, any more than it matters whether Ronsard's sonnet on the death of "Marie" is inspired by a real loss or by a patron's commission. In Batyushkov's case, his Riga love, whether real or imaginary, gave us the most moving (and the most shapely) of his early poems:

CONVALESCENCE

As the white lily feels the mower's murderous scythe
    And bows its head, slowly dissolving,
So in my illness I could sense untimely death
    And thought the hand of fate was on me.
The black of Erebus already veiled my sight,
    My heart was beating time more slowly,
I was dissolving, vanishing, still young, the sun
    Of my existence setting.
But you came close to where I lay, life of my soul,
    Your rose-red lips, so sweetly breathing,
The tears that sparkled in the brightness of your eyes
    And the succession of your kisses,
Your burning sighs, the power of your beloved words,
    All called upon me to abandon
The dark domains of grief, the fields of death, the shores
    Of Lethe, for the world of passion.
You gave me back my life; this was your blessed gift.
    From now on I shall breathe you only,
Even the hour of torment will seem sweet to me,
    And love will be my dissolution.

(Essays, 214)

In the autumn of 1807, when the militia was disbanded, Batyushkov joined the Guards, but he very soon fell ill and spent the winter in St. Petersburg on sick leave, being looked after by the Olenin family. Over the next year, moving to and fro between the capital and his northern homeland, he was preoccupied with family affairs and relations with his father and sisters. His decision to join the army had upset his father, who then exacerbated relations by remarrying. Konstantin's unmarried sisters Aleksandra and Varvara took their brother's side in the quarrel, and they eventually went with him to live on his mother's estate at Khantonovo, but only when he was able to inherit it at the age of twenty-one. Meanwhile, he seems to have written very little, though he was continuing to work on the translation of Tasso. He did, however, write one more verse epistle to Gnedich, enclosed with a letter of July 1, 1808, sounding the note of country boredom, isolation, and depression, which will so often be heard in his letters:

> Now I can break the chain of silence
> And greet my bosom friend again.
> It's a long time since last I sent you
> The scratchings of my idle pen.
> And how can my flute make tuneful music
> Beneath this empty, savage sky?
> Is this a place for the young muses
> To come and make sweet poetry?
> How can I sing oppressed by fate,
> Held fast by a cruel destiny,
> With neither friends nor family?
>
> Amid a sea of desolation
> Only cold hearts can take their ease
> And cast their eyes without emotion

On tombs of loved ones and of friends,
On death and malicious calumny
That like a serpent, basely writhing,
Inflicts a cruel wound in hiding
On spotless innocence itself;
But with a soul that feels so deeply
Can I remain a placid victim
In this harsh world of calumny?
On this earth we all will find
An open grave for humankind,
Where, mown down by the fatal scythe,
They all must fall, the sceptered tsar,
The shepherd, monk and warrior!
Can I alone deserve to live
In happiness, eternally?

Alas, we all bow down beneath
The fetters and the yoke of grief,
Which all our lives we're doomed to bear
With arms too weak to cast them off.
But how, dear friend, can we endure them
And never weep or feel despair?
It's simpler far to cross the ocean
When Boreas spreads his wings in anger
Unharmed in a frail cockleshell
Bereft of rudder, shroud and sail
And never lift your eyes to heaven.

Now in your company I weep
While, lightning-like, time flashes by.
The bright moon shining over me
Stares peacefully into the lake;

All is asleep in night's May shadow,
The waterfall is barely heard,
The groves in the quiet valley slumber,
And through their branches overhead
The subtle moonbeams float to earth,
And I, in Morpheus' mighty hand,
Break off my flute's sorrowful tune—
Perhaps before this short night ends
In the land of dreams I'll find you
And once again embrace you, friend.

(CP, 81–82)

Then, in the autumn of 1808, his regiment was sent off on a new campaign. As an indirect result of the treaties signed at Tilsit, Russia went to war with Sweden over the possession of Finland, which was achieved in September 1809. For him the campaign lasted about eight months, during which he spent a hard winter in the northern part of Finland. The wildness of the country had a romantic appeal, and after his return to Russia he exploited this in his first serious prose writing, an "Extract from the Letters of a Russian Officer in Finland," first published in the journal *The European Herald* (Vestnik Evropy) in 1810. It opens with the words:

I have seen a country close to the Pole, bordering on the Hyperborean sea, where nature is poor and cheerless, where the sun gives continual warmth for two months only, but where, as in countries more blessed by nature, people can find happiness.

(Essays, 95)

Then come poetic descriptions of northern scenery, the vast and impenetrable forests, the silence and darkness, the granite cliffs and roaring torrents, the interminable snowbound winters, the howling wolves and wheeling birds of prey. And this wild "Hyperborean" land once had wild inhabitants, warriors who drank blood out of the skulls of their enemies. Mingling images from Norse mythology with the poems of Ossian and even Arthurian legend, Batyushkov writes of the dreams of the poet in such a landscape:

> Perhaps on this pine-covered cliff, at whose foot a gentle breeze stirs the deep waters of the gulf, perhaps on this cliff stood a temple to Odin. Here the poet loves to dream of bygone days and to plunge in thought into those ages of barbarism, magnanimity and fame. Here he looks with pleasure on the ocean waves once covered with the ships of Odin, Arthur and Harald, on the dark horizon where the shades of vanished warriors passed, on the stones, relics of gray antiquity, on which can be seen mysterious signs, drawn by some unknown hand.
>
> *(Essays, 98)*

This is followed by a long quotation from Batyushkov's youthful poem "Dreaming," and finally by a picturesque evocation of the Russian army encamped in this wilderness.

Such is the romantic aspect of the northern campaign, later echoed in rather derivative poems such as "The Scald" and "Warriors' Dream." Batyushkov's correspondence conveys a less heroic image. The campaign alternated between periods of movement and action (some of it shared with his friend Petin, who was soon wounded in the leg and separated from him), and long weeks spent in camps in the freezing wastes of northern Finland. Plagued by illness and longing to get back to St. Petersburg, Batyushkov wrote to Olenin:

> It's so cold here that time's wings have frozen. Dreadful monotony. Boredom stretches out on the snow, or to put it more simply, it is so depressing in this savage, barren wilderness without books or

society, and often without wine, that we can't tell a Wednesday from
a Sunday. So most humbly I beg you to order for me a Tasso (whom
I have had the misfortune to lose) and a Petrarch . . .

(WP, 77)

The letter speaks again of *skuka*, a very Russian term, translated
here as "boredom," but really a more all-embracing world weari-
ness; this was a constantly lurking presence in Batyushkov's life.
Against *skuka*, one remedy was Italian poetry. During the Finnish
campaign he was continuing work on his translation of Tasso. In
letters to Gnedich, he more than once asks himself why he should
devote so much time to a task that would bring few rewards. How-
ever, in 1808 he published in a journal some of Canto 1 of *Jerusalem
Delivered* (La Gerusalemme liberata), together with a rather formal
epistle "To Tasso." This piece was inspired by the "Épître au Tasse"
of the French poet La Harpe, who also translated Tasso and whose
admiration and sympathy for the suffering poet found a ready echo
in Batyushkov. His own epistle may be derivative both in form
(rhyming alexandrine couplets) and in sentiment, but it announces
some of the characteristic directions his later poetry will take. The
extracts given below concern Tasso's many-sided poetic gift, his suf-
ferings at the hand of ill-wishers, and his continuing fame:

> . . . Torquato, he who knows the bitter taste
> Of love and sorrow and in his young days,
> Following the muse, enters the hall of fame,
> He suffers and is great before his time!
> You sang, and all Parnassus woke in rapture,
> Young Phoebus with the muses in Ferrara
> Placed in your hands the lyre of Ovid's songs,
> Sheltering your genius with immortal wings.
> You sang the noise of war—the pallid furies

Spread out for you its darkness and its horrors:
Men race over the field, trampling on banners,
Their fury burning with the torch of hatred,
Hair flying in the wind and bloodied tunics,
And I see deaths . . . with brazen Mars beside me . . .
But war and horror, the clash of swords and spears,
The voice of Mars, have vanished into air;
I hear far off the oaten pipes of shepherds,
And I can give myself to other passions:
No hatred now, but the young god of love
Sleeps softly in a flowery myrtle grove.
And then he rises—once again swords glitter!
What Proteus so changes you, Torquato,
What wondrous god has filled these holy dreams
With both a grim and tender beauty's beams?
. . . .

And what reward, Torquato, were you given
For your harmonious songs? The critics' venom,
The courtiers' flattery and false words of praise,
Enough to poison any poet's days.
And cruel love, the source of all your troubles,
Appeared before you in those golden chambers,
And from her hands you took the poisoned cup
Entwined with flowers and roses still in bud,
You drank it all, and in a dream of love
Enslaved yourself, enslaved your lyre to beauty.
But joys are false and happiness is fleeting—
The veil is torn. You are a slave, Torquato!
Thrown into darkness, like a criminal,
Deprived of freedom and of Phoebus' light.
The poet's soul is broken by deep sadness,

His talent, his creative power have vanished,
His reason's gone! . . . O you whose treachery
Plunged Tasso in a hell of cruelty,
Come, feast your eyes on this fine entertainment,
And revel in the ruin of his talent!
Come! He who was above all human praise,
Who gave his heroes eloquence, whose eyes
Pierced through the clouds into the heavenly mansions—
Here groans in chains. . . . O you great Gods, have mercy!
How long yet must he, guiltless, bear the weight
Of shameful envy and infernal spite?

. . . .

Godlike poet, we call to you in vain,
But the whole world still rings with Tasso's fame!
All that is left of Troy is dust and ashes,
We cannot tell where her great men are buried,
Divine Skamander eddies endlessly,
But in the minds of men, Homer still lives,
And humankind still glory in their singer:
His shrine—the world. And yours too will survive us.

(*CP, 83–85*)

Eventually Batyushkov's requests for leave were successful and he was allowed to return to Russia. Much of the second half of 1809 was spent in the country, in the still-neglected estate at Khantonovo, in the company of his two unmarried sisters. Although this was the place of his household gods, he was not happy there, constantly short of money, and often ill and depressed. As he put it in a letter to Gnedich (in words that seem ominous in hindsight), "the charming, beautiful Madame de Sévigné says that if she could only live two hundred years, she would become a perfect woman. If I live another ten years, I shall go mad. Really, life is tedious and there's no consolation" (*SP*, 286). But in fact he did find consolation in reading and writing. This period of enforced solitude gave Batyushkov the leisure to extend his already impressive literary culture and to work out his own poetic values and strategies.

His reading was extensive and covered several different literatures: the poets of Rome and of the Italian Renaissance, the writings of Voltaire and Rousseau, some English writers, as well as contemporary Russian writing. As we saw in chapter 1, he was strongly influenced by French love poetry of the late eighteenth century, notably that of Évariste de Parny. Admiration led to translation, which led to original writing. Translation is particularly important for literary cultures that are just finding their own voice, as Russian culture was in the early nineteenth century. The great translators of the time were Gnedich and in particular Vasily Zhukovsky, whom Batyushkov was soon to meet in Moscow, but translation and imitation occupy a central position in Batyushkov's oeuvre too. Before long, he would be seen as the Russian Parny, and already in Khantonovo he was beginning his free translation of Parny's *Madagascar Songs* (Chansons madécasses).

Parny, born on the Île Bourbon (present-day Réunion), was vastly popular in his day—Chateaubriand described him as "the only elegiac poet France has produced."[3] He became famous with his *Erotic Poems* (Poésies érotiques, 1778), followed a few years later by the *Madagascar Songs*, prose poems supposedly based on the folk songs of Madagascar (comparable in a way to Macpherson's recent versions of Gaelic poetry in Biblical English). Since Parny probably never set foot in Madagascar, there is some doubt about the status of his versions, but this didn't prevent them from attracting, like Ossian, foreign readers and translators. Only one of Batyushkov's Madagascan songs survives, in which he recasts Parny's poetic prose into rhyming quatrains. Parny's poem (Chanson VIII) begins:

Il est doux de se coucher durant la chaleur sous un arbre touffu, et
d'attendre que le vent du soir amène la fraîcheur.
(It is sweet to lie during the heat under the dense foliage of a tree
and to wait for the evening breeze to bring coolness.)

In Batyushkov's poem this gives a quatrain that can be translated:

How sweet to sleep in the cool shade
While the great heat consumes the valley
And the wind in this forest glade
Stirs the leaves with its soft breathing.

(CP, 117)

Batyushkov was to translate quite a few more Parny poems in the
following year or two; I shall return to these and other translations
in the next chapter.

He composed a number of other poems in these Khantonovo
months, most of them concerned with the campaign of 1807.
These include two we have already looked at, "Memories of
1807" and "Convalescence," as well as a nostalgic epistle to Count
Wielgorski, a Polish composer he had met in Riga. Here too we can
probably place an "Answer to Gnedich," a short verse epistle in his
familiar manner replying to a friendly letter, painting a formalized
self-portrait of the poet as modest country-dweller, and reflecting
on the rival pull of friendship and love.

ANSWER TO GNEDICH

Now and in time to come, dear Gnedich,
Your friend gives you his hand and heart;
He has served his time with the blind goddess,
Mother of cares that bear no fruit.

Alas! my friend, in my young season
I too fell foul of Circe's charms,
But looking in my empty pockets,
I have forsaken love and arms.
Let those afflicted with ambition
Hurl fire and thunderbolts with Mars
While I, not seeking recognition,
Live happy in my little house.
There let us place our clay Penates
Together in a friendly shade
And then sit down to simple suppers—
Our dreams will give us golden days.
And if by chance love should come calling
On our retreat, friendship's abode,
Alas! your friend, the same as ever,
Will pay his homage to the god.
As a guest, overcome by feasting,
Gets up and quits the sumptuous board,
So I, lost in a lover's rapture,
Uncaringly will quit the world!

(Essays, 274)

All the poems and letters sent to Gnedich failed to persuade him to come and stay in Khantonovo. At his friend's request, however, Batyushkov wrote some verses to a "goddess of beauty," the great tragic actress and singer Ekaterina Semyonova (who provides yet another link with *War and Peace*, since she sings in the opera attended by Natasha and so memorably described by Tolstoy). At the same time, soon after his return to Khantonovo, he was beginning to write in a more acid vein on the cultural life of St. Petersburg and Moscow, about which he was well informed, even though living at a distance. In August, he sent Gnedich some newly composed epigrams, including this "Madrigal for a New Sappho:"

> You are Sappho, I Phaon, I agree:
> But it's a great sorrow to me
> That you don't know the way to the sea.

(Essays, 306)

Referring to Sappho's legendary death by drowning, this is directed, no doubt unfairly, against the poet Anna Bunina, possibly referring to her love for the poet Ivan Dmitriev. Batyushkov admired Dmitriev and was later on good terms with Bunina; the main reason for his malice at this time was no doubt her alliance with the traditionalist camp of writers led by Admiral Shishkov. The Shishkovists were the main targets in the long satirical poem, "Vision on the Banks of Lethe" (1809), which was to make Batyushkov a fashionable figure in the metropolitan literary world.

Russian literature at this time was broadly split into two camps. The most prominent figure was Nikolay Karamzin (born 1766), now best known as the author of the great *History of the Russian State*, but in the years around 1800 seen principally as a reformer of the Russian literary language and the leader of the sentimentalist movement, which found expression in his periodical, the *Moscow Journal* (Moskovsky zhurnal). He and his numerous disciples (many of them based in Moscow) aimed to reform the language of Russian literature, reducing the number of Slavonicisms (expressions based on the archaic language of the Russian church), inventing new terms often based on French models, so as to create an easy, elegant, modern style, suitable for use in light society verse. This tendency was opposed by the conservative camp whom we now call the Archaists, grouped around the poet, statesman, and admiral Aleksandr Shishkov. In a *Discourse on the Old and New Style* published in 1803,

Shishkov had criticized the modernizing cosmopolitanism of the Karamzinians. A believer in the classical poetics of eighteenth-century Russia, he championed Church Slavonic as the root of Russian, but also advocated the traditional language of the peasants as an additional source for literary Russian. In the "Vision on the Banks of Lethe," Batyushkov coins the new word "Slavenophile" to describe Shishkov; the conflict between these two camps can be seen as a literary prefiguration of the Slavophile/Westernizer debates that were to be so important in nineteenth-century Russian culture.

Although he was later prominent as a critic of the Archaists, Batyushkov is not the champion of any one cause in the "Vision," but shoots his arrows in all directions in a long satire that owes a good deal to French models. He avoids mentioning Karamzin, but the Moscow Karamzinians get their share of mockery. The basic notion of the satire is a dream in which all the currently active poets are struck dead by Apollo and have to come before a jury of the great dead poets; they throw their works into the waters of Lethe, the river of oblivion—those that sink will be forgotten. Here come the Karamzinians, sporting a variety of sentimental affectations, most of them easily identified by knowledgeable contemporary readers (the toupee-wearing "prince of fibbers" is the Karamzinian poet Shalikov):

> But here appeared some other shadows;
> They hailed from Moscow's white-walled town
> And sported wonderful apparel:
> Their robes were copiously sewn
> With leaves from head to foot; one gloried
> In childish verse and childish prose,
> One in a mausoleum, a churchyard,
> One in the diary of his soul;
> Some sang Melania, Ziulmisa,
> The Moon or Vesper or a dove,

Glafira, Chloe, Militrisa,
Or rams, or cats and toms in love.
All these in melancholy verse
In every key, for *charming* ears
(O age of iron!). But the ladies
Had never once in sleep or waking
Noticed these miserable bards.
In all the pallid, doleful crowds,
One sporting a well-combed toupee,
A prince of fibbers, licensed poet,
Presents his new work to the court.
"And who are you?" "Alas, a shepherd,
A sigher, never taken short;
Here is my crook, my wreath of flowers,
Here my taffeta bouquet,
And here the list of stubborn beauties
For whom I lived and breathed all day,
And whom I wearied with my charms.
Here is my Aglaya, my sheep"—
He spoke and, yawning wearily,
Fell into Lethe half-asleep.

(Essays, 358–59)

The next victim is rather different. It is the poet Sergey Glinka, who was later to become a good friend of Batyushkov, in spite of the lines about him in the "Vision." In his journal *Russian Herald* (Russky vestnik), he was a champion of all things Russian, which exasperated the more cosmopolitan, though patriotic, Batyushkov:

"Ouf, I'm so tired! A chair, your honor—
I'm very famous, let me sit;
I am immortal when I'm funny."

"Your name?" "*A Russian and a poet.*
I chase after celebrity,
Foreign good sense is my enemy.
To Russians my twisted words are straight.
And by my pilgrim's scrip I swear it."
"But who are you?" "The Russian Rousseau,
The Russian Young, Locke and Racine.
I have composed three Russian dramas
For Russians: I have no more strength
To write more tearful plays for Russians.
My labors have been all in vain.
These foreign notions are to blame."
With that, he vanished in the stream.

(Essays, 359)

Eventually it is the turn of Shishkov and his team, the devotees of
noble Russian antiquity:

And then, on Hades' sullen shore,
Appeared a great and wondrous spirit.
In a stupendous coach of yore
He quietly approached the river;
Instead of nags between the shafts
People were harnessed fore and aft,
And with a will they heaved and pulled him,
And in his wake like autumn drones
Thronging the air in light-winged squadrons
Shades of all kinds came floating on
To left and right. At the sound "Whoa!"
The pale shade shook his weary brow
And came out coughing from the carriage.
"And who might you be?" Minos queried,

"And who are these?" to which the shade
Answered: "From Neva's banks we hail—
All Russian bards." "But what misfortune
Has changed these people into horses?"
"This is my youthful regiment
Of poets fired by love of plaudits;
They sang Pozharsky and they lauded
The venerable Hermogen.
Their thoughts are aimed at heaven, their words
Are taken from the Holy Scripture,
Their lines may be a little rough,
But genuine Varyago-Russian."
"And you yourself?" "I too am one
Whom old Kurganov[4] taught to write;
I did not deal in trifles, but
In patience, sweat and noble toil,
For I am a *Slavenophile*."

(*Essays, 360–61*)

But though a comic figure, Shishkov is in a different league from his followers, and he and his works will escape drowning: "for his firm mind and his deeds he tasted the reward of immortality."

The strongest approbation, however, is given to the eccentric figure of the "Russian La Fontaine," the fable writer Ivan Krylov, a writer set apart from both camps, and always the object of Batyushkov's affectionate mockery and real admiration:

A shade now came to Minos' throne,
Unkempt and in the strangest costume,
Wrapped in a tattered dressing gown,
All fluffy, with a shaggy forehead,

Carrying a napkin and a book,
Saying: "Death deliberately took
Me unawares one day at table,
But I am ready, when you like,
To start again with you and sample
Hell's offering of pies and wine:
Now is the time, good friends, to dine.
You know me, Krylov is my name!"
"Krylov! Krylov!" they all exclaim,
That band of shades, echoed above
By all the vaults of Hell: "Krylov!"
"Come and sit down, good friend, and tell us,
How are you feeling?" "Could be worse."
"And what have you been doing?" "Just trifles—
Keeping my head down, letting time pass,
And mostly sleeping, drinking, eating—
Here you are, Minos, here are my works;
I didn't bring a lot of writing:
Some comedies and some light verse,
And fables—throw them in the water!"
Lo! they all floated up, and soon
Krylov, life's miseries forgotten,
Went straight to heaven to dine at noon.

More sights met my imagination,
But have you really got the patience
To hear my visions to the end?
It is unwise to gossip, friends—
Someone I know might be offended:
So—the least said, the soonest mended.

(Essays, 362–63)

And so the "Vision" ends. It did indeed give offense, particularly to the Shishkovists, and Batyushkov refused to let it be published. Before long he was reconciled to some of his victims. He had intended it for a small circle of friends and was rather alarmed when in St. Petersburg Gnedich read it and named its author to the very sociable Olenin, but by then it was too late. The poem was not published until 1841, but in 1810 it circulated in numerous handwritten copies and brought its author an instant reputation. The light rhyming verse (very different from his more ponderous youthful imitations of Boileau), the impudence, the fantasy and the wit of the satire quickly became canonical, and were imitated by many younger poets. One of its first admirers was a new friend, the young poet Vyazemsky, whose praise was so fulsome that Batyushkov, even though he was pleased with his poem, replied with another of his airy epistles:

> Flatterer of my lazy muse,
> You have created new-forged fetters
> For me to carry now that you
> Have transformed my sleepy Lethe
> Into Jordan's noble stream
> And in laughter swung a censer
> Spreading such a heady incense
> That in an enraptured dream
> I, forgetting poetry,
> Nodded off and saw a vision:
> Laughing friend, I dreamt that bright
> Phoebus had me in his sights,
> Dragged me to the dismal river
> With my poems every one,
> And drowned them *in oblivion.*

(CP, 245–46)

This ends on a self-deprecating joke, but the notion of drowning in the river of oblivion—perhaps an allusion to Derzhavin's great fragment on the all-consuming river of time[5]—had serious overtones for someone as concerned with literary fame as Batyushkov. It was to reappear in some of the last poems he wrote.

THE CITY AND THE COUNTRY

03

Some time in 1810 Batyushkov wrote an essay (unpublished until 1986) about the advantages of solitude and society for the poet. He concedes that polite society teaches the manners and bon ton that a writer needs in an enlightened age, and that Virgil and Ovid lived in the palaces of Augustus, but he himself takes a more Rousseauist view of the bad effects of city life on the poet:

> Experience of the world, knowledge of etiquette and of manners, society manners, which are as different from the manners of bardic times as the heroes of Homer are from Prussian generals; in a word, all this worldly wisdom dries up the heart and soul, and it is they that are the true and inexhaustible sources of poetry.
>
> *(SP, 38)*

The society of fellow poets is essential of course, but ideally this should be combined with country solitude. Poetry thrives in a peaceful retreat.

In practice, Batyushkov was fully aware of the advantages and drawbacks of both the busy city and the quiet country. The city might be endlessly distracting, but rural solitude—in his case usually Khantonovo—could be desperately tedious. Though he was glad to escape the capitals, his attachment to the Lares and Penates of his estate was largely forced upon him by lack of funds. His tendency to dissatisfaction and *skuka* seems to have been rooted deep inside him; although partly hidden by his Epicurean posture, it comes to the surface again and again in his letters to Gnedich and other friends. Between 1807 and 1821, he was constantly on the move.

At the end of 1809, perhaps buoyed up by the success of the "Vision," he went to live for the first time in Moscow, as a welcome guest of Ekaterina Fyodorovna, the widow of Mikhail Muravyov (who had died in 1807). The city was very different from St. Petersburg; a letter written to Gnedich a few weeks after his arrival shows Batyushkov still reeling under the mass of new impressions. He finds Moscow hard going at first:

> I am very solitary here. I don't play cards. I see just walls and people. Moscow is an ocean for me: not a single house except for my own, not a single corner where I can unburden myself with a friend. My only consolation is Petin: he's a really good fellow. I sit by the fire and chat with him, and time passes somehow.
>
> *(SP, 295)*

In spite of such characteristically melancholy notes, Batyushkov did get out and about and saw a lot of the city and its inhabitants. Rather than describing it in letters, he accumulated notes that together make up "Strolls Through Moscow," a fascinating prose text that remained unpublished in his lifetime. It is a precious glimpse of the city before the great fire of 1812, written in a free, casual way (on the model of letters to friends). The author is a disengaged spectator on the Addisonian model, but equally a predecessor of the Baudelairean *flâneur* in the city. This is the persona he describes in a letter to Gnedich of November 1811: "an idler, a joker, an oddball, a carefree child, a scribbler of verse" (*SP*, 322). Similarly, at the beginning of "Strolls Through Moscow," he writes:

> My second reason [for not writing to his friend] is idleness, a very powerful reason! So in passing, going from house to house, from promenade to promenade, from supper to supper, I shall write a few notes on the city and the life of its inhabitants, disordered and disconnected notes, but you will read them with pleasure as they will remind you of your good friend.
>
> (*Essays, 379*)

His attitude toward Moscow society is satirical, sometimes affectionate, sometimes less so. His sharply drawn pictures prefigure the realistic but heightened descriptions of a Gogol or a Leskov. Above all, he stresses the enormous contrasts in a city where luxury and misery live shockingly side by side:

> A strange juxtaposition of ancient and extremely modern building, of poverty and wealth, of European and Asiatic manners. A marvelous, incomprehensible fusion of fussiness, vanity and genuine glory and grandeur, of ignorance and enlightenment, politeness and barbarism.
>
> (*Essays, 380*)

And within this strange, labyrinthine world, he picks out particular scenes and characters. Here is Tverskoy Boulevard, at the time a place where society folk went to see and be seen:

> What strange outfits, what faces! Here is an officer from Moldavia, the grandson of an ancient court beauty and the heir of a gouty old gentleman, both of whom can't take their eyes off his brightly colored uniform and his childish pranks; here is a provincial dandy

who has come to pick up the latest fashions and is feasting his eyes on a lucky individual who has just arrived posthaste from the banks of the Seine in blue breeches and a large and shapeless frock coat. Here a beauty is being followed by a crowd of worshippers, there an old general's wife is chattting to a neighbor, and alongside them a weighty, pensive tax-farmer, who firmly believes that god created half the human race to be distillers and the other half to be drunks, struts slowly along with his beautiful wife and his little spaniel. A university professor in a gown that would be a credit to the late Crates,[1] makes his way home or to his dusty lecture room. A merry fellow sings vaudeville songs and sets his poodle on the passersby, while an inveterate poet recites an epigram and waits for applause or an invitation to dinner. Such is the pleasure-ground I have been visiting every day, almost always with some new pleasure. The complete freedom to walk up and down with whoever you meet, the great concourse of familiar and unfamiliar people, all this has always had a special appeal for idlers, people with nothing to do, and people who like observing faces. I belong to the first and last of these categories.

(Essays, 385)

Batyushkov enjoyed being a spectator in the great theatre of the world, then, but what really mattered to him was the society of writers and poets, and he was very soon in the thick of it. As early as January 1810, he wrote to his sister: "I have made the acquaintance of all the local Parnassus except Karamzin, who is dreadfully ill. I've never seen such a collection of faces" (*WP*, 94). In fact, he met Karamzin by chance in the street not long after this, and found a good friend in him. As for the "collection of faces," some of these were the poets he had mocked in the "Vision on the Banks of Lethe"—and with most of these he was soon on good terms. But there were two poets in Moscow who became his close friends: Prince Pyotr Vyazemsky and Vasily Zhukovsky.

Vyazemsky, whom we have already met giving what seemed to Batyushkov excessive praise to the "Vision," was himself to become (in Joseph Brodsky's words) "a superb yet underestimated poet,"[2] a central figure in the "Pushkin Pléiade." As such he was the dedicatee of Evgeny Baratynsky's great collection *Half-light*, in which he is described as the "star of our scattered constellation."[3] He lived to the age of eighty-six; in his later years, he was close to court circles, holding influential positions in the civil service, including the censor's office, and his views became more conservative—indeed he seemed to the new radical intelligentsia a reactionary figure from another age. In 1810, however, he was barely eighteen, five years Batyushkov's junior, the cosmopolitan descendant of a rich and ancient noble family. He was a young man-about-town and a free spirit, witty and combative, publishing rebellious verse in the underground press, a great enthusiast for contemporary French writing—though he was soon to become actively involved in the struggle against Napoleon, fighting at Borodino. Some years later, Batyushkov sent to Vyazemsky a little poem about a new portrait of a friend whom he knew as a carefree lover of pleasure:

> Who is this with the knotted brows,
> Gloomy and tousled like Theodulus?
> Amazing! it is our own Catullus,
> Our Vyazemsky, the bard of love and mirth.

> (*Essays, 373*)

Vyazemsky and Batyushkov sympathized immediately. With Vasily Zhukovsky, who was Batyushkov's senior by four years, there seems to have been a brief testing period, but soon the three poets formed a close-knit group of friends and allies. In 1812, having witnessed the battle of Borodino, Zhukovsky was to shoot to fame with his patriotic hymn "A Bard in the Camp of Russian Warriors," but even in 1810 he had a literary reputation in Moscow. He was the editor of the Karamzinian *European Herald* (Vestnik Evropy), where some of Batyushkov's early work was published. Whereas Batyushkov was much influenced by French and Italian poetry, Zhukovsky was a voice of northern Romanticism, a devotee of English and German poetry. As early as 1802 he had published what was to become a vastly influential translation of Gray's "Elegy Written in a Country Churchyard"—it was above all as a translator that he influenced Russian poetry. Around the time when Batyushkov got to know him, he became famous for his ballads, mainly derived from German sources; Batyushkov addressed him as a "hermit" in an epistle sent in a letter of June 1812, but later changed this to "balladeer."

In the summer of 1810, the three poets went off to stay at Vyazemsky's country residence at Ostafievo, not far outside Moscow. This splendid neoclassical palace later received many writers, including Pushkin; here, too, Karamzin spent many years writing his *History of the Russian State*. Batyushkov plunged with pleasure into this patrician luxury, but then, after three weeks, he suddenly left for Khantonovo. From here he wrote apologetically to his friends—thus to Zhukovsky:

> I left you *en impromptu*, went off like Aeneas, like Theseus, like Ulysses from the wh——s (because my presence was needed here in the country, because I got to feel gloomy, very gloomy in Moscow, because I was scared of being bewitched by you, my funny friends)
>
> (*SP, 300–301*)

It was a strange move, perhaps partly financial in origin, but corresponding to Batyushkov's inability to settle in one place. And if he had been "gloomy" in Moscow, he was soon bored in the country—or rather, he oscillated between enjoyment and boredom. What is more, he was plagued by illness; his health, never very robust, had been affected by his wound at Heilsberg and the hardships of the Finnish campaign. He wrote to Zhukovsky in the letter cited above: "I am so ill, so weak now, that I can neither write nor think," and the same note would recur constantly in the following years. At the same time, he tried hard to cure himself, and wrote repeatedly of his desire to find some useful and honorable service in the capital. Gnedich was keen to assist him and eventually helped him to a post in the public library of St. Petersburg. But for the moment, Batyushkov appeared to be the slave of illness and idleness. When Gnedich reproached him with this, he replied with a mocking description of his full country days: ten or twelve hours in bed sleeping and dreaming, one hour smoking, one hour getting dressed, three hours of dolce far niente, one hour for dinner, one hour digesting, quarter of an hour watching the sun set, three quarters of an hour for "natural needs," one hour remembering friends (including half an hour for Gnedich), one hour with his dogs, half an hour reading Tasso, half an hour repenting that he has translated him, three hours yawning and waiting for nightfall. Then, more seriously, he wrote: "I am very bored here, I want to enter the service, I need to change my way of life—but what comes of it? Like a certain oriental sage, I am waiting for some goddess to fly in from some star . . ." (*WP* 113–14). In other words, he settled for dreams.

The same pattern of existence continued into 1811. Most of the first half of the year was spent in Moscow, enjoying the city's many distractions and entertainments as well as the rich literary life. Gnedich did not approve, thinking that the frivolities of the city were luring Batyushkov away from his true vocation. And then again, in midsummer, money ran out and the poet settled in Khantonovo, again prey to *skuka* and melancholy. He wrote to Gnedich in August:

> Me—a dreamer? On the contrary! I am bored and like you I very often say: People are all swine, I am a person, therefore . . . finish the sentence yourself. Where is happiness? Where is pleasure? Where is peace? Where is that pure heartfelt voluptuousness in which my heart loved to plunge itself? It has all flown away, vanished with the songs of Chaulieu, the voluptuous dreams of Tibullus and the charming Gresset, the airy nymphs of Anacreon.
>
> *(SP, 310)*

But this was perhaps more a passing mood than a permanent state. Batyushkov did not lose touch with the poets who had consoled him; indeed, he spent much of his time in Khantonovo plunged in books. In 1810, in a notebook given to him by Zhukovsky, he jotted down thoughts, many of them reading notes, referring to the Roman poets and historians, Enlightenment French culture, Tasso, the Scandinavian *Edda*, and much else. There are several pages on Horace, whose epistolary style is echoed in his own verse, and in whom he probably saw a kindred spirit, "afflicted with the incurable disease of those on whom fortune heaps gifts early on—*satiety*." He quotes the Roman poet as saying: "When I am at Tivoli I want to be in Rome; when in Rome, I want to be at Tivoli," and comments: "That's what the happiest of all poets wrote, a man whom fortune cherished as her special favorite" (*SP*, 246–48). He did not see himself as fortune's favorite, it is true, but he must have recognized in himself the desire for constant change. Among modern writers, Batyushkov is especially attached to Montaigne:

> That's a book I shall keep reading all my life! . . . You could call it a very learned book, a very entertaining book, a very profound

book; it is never tiring, always new, in a word it is the history and the romance of the human heart. Montaigne can be compared with Homer.

(SP, 244)

The fruits of his reading figure in letters to Gnedich, Vyazemsky, and Zhukovsky, where he comments critically or enthusiastically on what is appearing in the capitals, as well as on what Goethe would soon be calling "world literature." These letters to friends are real works of art, frequently prefiguring the new kind of poetry that Batyushkov was writing. They are written from the heart, with frequent complaints about illness, boredom, poverty, and other woes, as we have seen. But they are also performances, full of zest, veering from familiarity to mock pomposity—the sort of letter that needs to be read aloud.

Take for instance a marathon letter written to Gnedich between November 27 and December 5, 1811. It begins with a long and impassioned reply to his friend's career advice, a defense of his freedom, and expression of his horror at the boredom of government service, before moving on to flippant inquiries about St. Petersburg literary life and detailed advice about finer points of prosody. Then comes a fresh start, no doubt provoked by rereading Gnedich's letter:

All writers, from Aristotle to Kachenovsky,[4] have constantly repeated: "Be precise in your choice of words—precise, precise, precise! Do not write *mouse* when you mean *house, sword* when you mean *word*, etc." But you, dear Nikolay, write unblushingly that I shall soon be thirty. You're wrong, wrong, wrong by six years, since there's no language where twenty-four equals thirty. What price precision? I for my part will not give up these six years, and like Alexander the Great I shall do many marvels in the great field . . . of our literature. In these six years I shall read all of Ariosto and translate a few pages of him, and in conclusion, reaching the age of thirty, I shall say with my poet:

Se a perder s'a libertá, non stimo
Il piu ricco capel, ch'in Roma sia.

(If it means losing my freedom, I place no value on the richest position in Rome.)

Since at thirty I shall be the same as I am now, an idler, a joker, an oddball, a carefree child, a scribbler but not a reader of verse; I shall be the same Batyushkov who loves his friends, falls in love out of boredom, plays cards having nothing better to do, fools around like a devil, thinks deeply like a little Dane, argues with everyone, but fights with no one, hates Slavs and Geoffroy the martyr, Tibullizes in his spare time and learns ancient geography so as not to forget that Rome is on the Tiber, which flows from north to south—and at thirty he'll be just the same, with just one difference, that now he calls you a friend of ten years' standing, and then there'll be five more, but to love you more, to feel greater friendship and affection for you is surely impossible. Farewell!

Then, after a break, he continues on December 5:

That's a long letter, you'll be saying! Don't be amazed! Tomorrow is your name day and I must congratulate you—which means adding a whole extra page. So, I congratulate you, dear friend, be happy, cheerful, wise, love me, poetry, and wine—*wine, our delight*, as your predecessor Kostrov[5] has it. But so that you always love poetry, wine, and me, your friend:

The gray-beard who is always flying,
Always coming, always going,
Here and there, and everywhere,

Dragging years and centuries,
Eating mountains, draining seas,
Giving life to the old world,
That old gray-beard, nature's pall,
Both desired and feared by all,
Winged and flighty—old man Time,
May he always in their prime
Keep the friendly ties you value,
And in spite of the world's folly
Bring to friendship's holy shore
Love and happiness galore!

Such is my wish—the same in prose or in verse. I permit you to write just as many verses for my name day and to drink my health with a bottle of . . . water, just as I shall do tomorrow, ceremoniously, with two noble witnesses, two friends of mine, two . . . curly-haired dogs.

Yesterday I received the volume of poetry edited by Zhukovsky. What a mess they have made of my poem "Remembering!" Lines missed out and rhymes left high and dry! Generally, I am happy with this edition, happy with your "Peruvian," happy with Voeikov's "Epistle on Nobility," happy with [Vasily] Pushkin, happy with Kantemir and Petrov, but even so, there's an ocean of rubbish! Guess what is beginning to annoy me? It's the Russian language and our authors, who treat it so mercilessly. And the language in itself is not too good, crude, with a whiff of the Tartar. Look at the letters and combinations of letters—Y, SHCH, SH, SHII, SHCHII, PRI, TRY! What barbarians! And the writers? But good luck to them! Forgive me for being cross with the Russian people and their language. I have just been reading Ariosto, breathing the pure air of Florence, reveling in the musical sonorities of the Italian language and conversing with the

> shades of Dante, Tasso and the mellifluous Petrarch, whose every
> word is a joy! Farewell!
>
> (*SP,* 322–24)

In spite of country tedium and ill health, this is Batyushkov in top
form, full of ideas and witticisms, enthusiasms and passions. It is
interesting to see him deploring the harsh sounds of Russian, the
very letters that would a century later be celebrated by Kruchonykh
and the Futurists as a refuge from overcivilized euphony.[6]

■ □ ■

Both in Moscow and in the country, he continued to write poems.
Several of these sprang from his reading, being either free trans-
lations or adaptations of his favorite poets. Indeed, it is striking
how many of his poems are derived from foreign models. Often
this is openly stated; in his poetic collection of 1817, three poems
are described as "from Parny" or "imitation of Parny," three are
attributed to Tibullus, and there are two "imitations" of the Ital-
ian poet Casti. In addition to this, however, there are at least ten
other free translations (from Parny, Millevoye, Bion, Schiller)—to
which one can add a number of free translations and imitations
not included in the 1817 volume, notably thirteen poems from the
Greek anthology.

If Batyushkov looked to foreign models, it was to enrich and
give direction to a still young poetic culture (the first great poet
in modern Russian, Lomonosov, preceded him by only two gen-
erations). Tibullus, Petrarch, Tasso, and Parny could offer Rus-
sian poets examples of lyrical feeling, elegant wit, and sonorous
beauty; at the same time, through translation, Batyushkov could
create his own individual voice, something different from existing
Russian poetry. In some cases, notably "My Penates," more than

one model provides the starting point. Sometimes, indeed, the impetus may come from a source that is not a poem at all. Take, for instance, this little piece inspired by a painting, Poussin's *Et in Arcadia ego*:

INSCRIPTION FOR A SHEPHERDESS'S TOMBSTONE

Dear friends, dear sisters, carelessly you play,
Frolicking, dancing, singing all the day.
I too like you once lived in Arcady
And in my tender years in groves and fields
  I tasted joy's too-fleeting gleam.
Love promised happiness in a golden dream;
But in that happy place what lay concealed?
  A tomb!

(Essays, 307)

In all cases, Batyushkov is what we can call a strong translator, reworking and using the original to make his own poem. In February 1810, sending Gnedich "The Apparition," a free translation of Parny's "Le Revenant," he comments: "I am sending you a little piece that I have taken, or rather conquered, from Parny. The idea is an original one. I don't think I've spoiled it in my translation . . ." (*SP*, 294–95). In French the poem begins with a sprightly vision of the poet's imminent death:

Ma santé fuit; cette infidèle
Ne promet pas de revenir,
Et la nature qui chancelle
A déjà su me prévenir
De ne pas trop compter sur elle.
Au second acte brusquement

Finira donc la comédie:
Vite je passe au dénouement;
La toile tombe, et l'on m'oublie.[7]

Batyushkov keeps close to Parny's form—the octosyllables become trochaic tetrameters, alternating lines of seven syllables with a masculine ending and lines of eight syllables with a feminine ending. This was a form he often used in his own poems—and which probably derives from French practice. The central ideas of the original are rendered too, but completely rephrased; Batyushkov plays down the theatrical metaphor of the last four lines, while building Parny's simple reference to "nature" into a darker classical scene starring Fate and Zeus. A quite close translation of his translation (though with rather looser rhyming) reads:

Look at me! I am just turning
Twenty, and my cheeks are pale;
Life's flower withers with the morning,
Fate has counted out my days,
Giving not a moment's grace.
Why delay? My groans and tears
Will not touch almighty Zeus,
And dark death, the final curtain,
Will fall, and I will be forgotten.

(*Essays*, 217)

A more developed translation is his version of Parny's "Persian Idyll" entitled "Le Torrent," the poem to which Mandelstam is referring when he writes of Zafna. The original is written in a poetic prose reminiscent of Ossian, but Batyushkov makes of this five well-formed stanzas. Even so, it is a relatively close translation, but again he feels free to omit, add, and embroider. The result in Russian reads like an original poem, the central theme being one that recurs throughout his work, the contrast of sensual happiness with the destructive river of time:

THE TORRENT

The storm is hushed, the sun makes its appearance
Far in the west, in the clear azure sky;
After the raging storm, a muddy torrent
Goes racing through the meadows noisily.
Zafna! come closer; for such a pure maiden
Under the palm trees' shade a rose bush grows,
While from the rocks and wilderness the torrent
Roars through the thickets, foaming as it goes.

You light these thickets with your presence, Zafna!
How sweet to be with you in this wilderness!
You sing to me of love in a soft whisper—
On quiet wings the wind bears off your voice.
Your voice, my Zafna, like the breath of morning
So full of sweetness, floats over flowers to me:
Torrent, be quieter, break off the seething
Roar of your waters foaming through the field.

Your voice, my Zafna, wakes an answering echo
Deep in my soul, I see your smile, your eyes
So full of joy . . . Maiden of love, I touched you,
Drank honey and roses from your moistened lips.
Is Zafna blushing? . . . Innocent companion,
Quietly press your lips on mine, unsealed . . .

And you, swift torrent of the wild expanses,
Roar gently as you foam across the field!

I sense the agitation in your bosom,
The beating of your heart, your tearful eyes;
How sweet the modest whispers of a maiden!
Zafna, o Zafna! see how as it flies
This fragrant flower is borne off by the current;
The waters hasten on—the flower is gone!
Time flows away more swiftly than this river
That downhill through the thickets roars and foams!

Time will destroy both youth and charming motion . . .
A smile lights up your face, maiden of love!
You feel your heart beat faster with emotion,
Fierce raptures and the ardor in the blood . . .
Zafna, o Zafna! the dove, all innocent,
And his still-loving mate envy our kiss . . .
Our sighs of love are borne off by the torrent
Roaring and foaming through the wilderness.

(Essays, 239–40)

Translation and the reworking of foreign poems occupied much
of Batyushkov's time in these years, but he wrote many lyric poems
of his own. One of his constant themes, from his earliest poems,
is the elegiac lament for lost youth and beauty, a notable exam-
ple being the short poem written in 1811 on the death of Varvara
Kokoshkina, the wife of an actor, and a close companion of Pyotr
Vyazemsky. Here Bayushkov uses an original stanzaic pattern with
feminine endings to bring into Russian something of the suavity he
so loved in Italian verse—emphasized here by the epigraph from
Petrarch:

ON THE DEATH OF THE WIFE OF F. F. KOKOSHKIN

Nell'età sua piú bella, e piú fiorita . . .
. . . E viva, e bella al ciel salita[8]

(Petrarch)

She is gone, our lovely Lila, sweet companion!
      All the world lies friendless!
Weep then, love and friendship, weep for sorrow, Hymen!
      Happiness has left us!

Friendship! every hour you filled her life with gladness,
      Flowers of celebration;
Weeping and lamenting, now you lay your goddess
      Where the grave lies waiting.

Now plant dismal yew trees, branches of sad cypress
      All around her relics!
Let the young folk bring their tears of purest sadness,
      Flowers with azure petals!

Everything is joyless, only the spring Zephyr
      Kisses her memorial;
Now death's quiet spirit, in this place of weeping,
      Steals the rose's glory.

Hymen, pale and mute here, in his long-drawn torment
      Is forever bound,
At the tomb he quenches his resplendent torchlight
      With a shaking hand.

(Essays, 241)

Friendship was a never-failing value for Batyushkov; his short poem of that name (quoted in chapter 1) is a free translation of Bion's Greek, made in 1811 or 1812. It is not surprising then that many of his poems are familiar verse epistles to friends, both male and female. The recipient of the following poem of 1809–1810 remains unknown—indeed it cannot be assumed that there was a real recipient, though the poem seems to carry genuine feeling:

FOR N'S BIRTHDAY

> O you who were the soul
> Of happiness and pleasure!
> You flowered like a rose
> Shining with heavenly beauty.
> Now all alone, neglected, sad, you sit
> Quietly by the window,
> Your birthday sees no songs, no compliments.
> But feel the heartfelt sympathy of friendship
> And let your beating heart be still.
> What have you lost? A swarm of flatterers,
> Scarecrows in mind, in dignity, in manners,
> Pitiless judges, tedious declaimers.
> You had one true friend . . . he is with you still.

(Essays, 230)

By contrast, everything suggests that "Elysium," written at about the same time and in the tripping trochaic meter used for many of the relaxed epistles to friends, is in fact a dream vision addressed to a woman of the poet's imagination, an imagination haunted by Horace and the French poets. Rather than talking to a real person, Batyushkov is weaving a variation on his theme of Epicurean enjoyment of life:

ELYSIUM

O, until your youth, so precious,
Like an arrow flies from you,
Drink joys from a brimming beaker,
And, when night falls, with the lute
Blend your voice in a sweet anthem,
Praising love and shunning care!
But when in our little cabin
Death comes for us, on our hour,
Then embrace me, hold me tightly
As the tendrils of the vine
Round the slender elm go winding—
So embrace me one last time!
Let your hands then, white as lilies
Bind me in a tender chain,
Bring your lips and mine together,
Pour your soul out like a flame!
By an unfamiliar pathway
Down there by the quiet shore
The good god of love will lead us
Through the meadows thick with flowers
To Elysium, where a blending
Of love and pleasure melts the soul
And once more the lover rises
With a new flame in his blood,
Where the nymphs, singing and wheeling
In a graceful choral dance
Gladden Horace, who for Delia
Still composes loving songs.
There, beneath the shifting shadow
Of the myrtles, love will braid

Wreathes for us, and tender poets
Greet us in the genial shade.

(*Essays, 341–42*)

As for male friends, apart from Gnedich, Vyazemsky, and Zhukovsky, there was his companion-in-arms, the young Ivan Petin, with whom he had already served in Prussia and Finland. In his letter of February 1810 (discussed earlier in this chapter), evenings by the fireside with Petin figured as Batyushkov's "only consolation" in an unfamiliar Moscow. Looking back on these days in his 1815 "Memories of Petin" (who had been killed in battle in 1813), he paints a homely scene:

> After the Swedish war was over, we both found ourselves in Moscow
> (1810). Petin, under treatment for serious wounds, devoted his spare
> time to the pleasures of society, whose charms are more intensely
> felt by military people than by others. Many an evening we spent by
> the fireside, deep in the satisfying conversations to which frankness
> and jollity give a particular charm.

(*Essays, 401–2*)

This is the background to an epistle to his friend, where Batyushkov embroiders memories of the battle of Indesalmi in Finland, before dwelling again on his failures and disappointments and concluding with the two comrades' remedy for all ills:

TO PETIN

Favorite of the god of battle!
Comrade in the ranks of Mars!
More than once we've paid a double
Tribute to glory in the wars:

Laurel on your noble helmet
Was intertwined with myrtle leaves,
While in a solitary corner
I picked forget-me-nots of love.
Do you remember, child of glory,
Indesalmi? Night of dread!
"Not for me such entertainments,"
I said—and with the muses fled!
While with bayonets you were driving
The Swedes beyond the distant wood,
I was heroically striving
To find for your return . . . some food.
Joking, you were always happy
In Aphrodite's lovely games,
But I am equally unhappy
In love and war, and wear away
My days of life in constant boredom
(O for a flash of happiness!).
I yawn at night, but in the morning
Weep for dreams and their caress.
Pointless tears! A chain awaits me
Woven from a skein of cares;
From my homeland I am driven
Once again on dangerous seas.
Blind Cupid steers my little vessel
Over the waves with a light hand,
And yawning indolence will settle
Herself beside me on the planks.
Perhaps one day, as youth too early
Races away from us, I may
Come to reason, but can joy really
Live with reason for a day?

But why am I in such a hurry,
Good friend, to sink behind a cloud?
My fate lies in the bottle, surely!
Let us drink and sing out loud:
"Happy the man who has made lovely
With flowers his love-haunted days,
Singing with carefree friends and comrades,
And found contentment—in his dreams!
Happy that man, his lot is better
Than all the tsars and their grandees.
Let us scorn slavery and fetters
And live in sweet obscurity,
Get through life one way or another,
Taking the rough days with the smooth,
Fill up our glass with wine, dear brother,
And laugh out loud at all the fools!"

(*Essays*, 280–81)

The sentiments expressed in the epistle to Petin are echoed in one of Batyushkov's most celebrated poems, "My Penates." Written in Khantonovo in the autumn of 1811, it is in part an apology for not accepting Vyazemsky's pressing invitations to return to Moscow for his wedding. The obstacle was of course a shortage of money, and Batyushkov replied very prosaically to Vyazemsky: "Alas! Like it or not, I must read my Horace and feed on hope, since the present is boring and stupid. I am living in the forests, deep in snow, surrounded by priests and Old Believers, weighed down with business" (*WP*, 125). But if he could not go to the city, he could imaginatively invite his friends to the country. The result was a poem of some three hundred lines, celebrating once again the pleasures of a visibly idealized humble home; the very place where Batyushkov suffered the agonies of *skuka* is transfigured, as if in a dream, into the refuge of friendship.

"My Penates" is written in the short rhyming lines favored by Batyushkov for this type of poem, in this case iambic trimeters. Like many of his poems, it combines different styles and tones, seeking for a personal voice rather than conformity to a set genre. Subtitled "An Epistle to Zh[ukovsky] and V[yazemsky]," it begins with an address to the classical household gods:

Penates of my fathers,
And household gods for me!
You own no golden treasures,
But you are content to be
In the dark cells and corners
Where here for my homecoming
I've quietly set you down
In places of your own;
Where I, a homeless wanderer,
Modest in what I wish for,
Have sought refuge from care.
You gods, receive my prayer
And give to me your blessing!
As a poet I bring no present
Of fragrant wines for you,
No cloud of incense, no!
But tears of soft emotion,
The heart's secret commotion
And the sweet songs that come
From the nine sisters' home.
O Lares! find a home here
In this unshowy house,

> Smile kindly on the poet
> And grant him happiness!
> Here in this humble hovel
> By the window, all forlorn,
> Stands a three-cornered table,
> Its cloth tattered and worn,
> And, hanging in the corner,
> A witness to old wars,
> There is the blunt, half-rusted
> Sword of my ancestors.
> Here are some chosen volumes
> And a bed rigid and hard,
> The plain kitchen utensils
> And cracked old pots and jars.
> Cracked! but to me they're dearer
> Than chaises longues draped in velvet
> Or the vases of the rich! . . .

The quiet country house is not a place for rustic labor, of course, but for love, friendship, and poetry. The poet's imagination peoples his solitude. He dreams of a visit from the enchanting Lila or Lileta, whose love and caresses make up for his failure to achieve glory. Friendship too is represented, especially the companionship of poets. Great figures from the past and present appear at his summons: Lomonosov, Derzhavin, Karamzin, Krylov, . . . Less conventionally, Batyushkov places at the end of his poem a direct address to his young poetic friends, once again rehearsing the Epicurean vision of life and death:

> O Lares and Penates
> Of this, my humble dwelling,
> Conceal from envious eyes

The happiness I cherish,
Conceal my deep contentment,
The peace and joy I prize!
Fortune, take back your presents
Of cares that dazzle sight!
With eyes full of indifference
I look at your swift flight;
Into a sheltered harbor
I've brought my little boat
And left the sons of fortune
To their unhappy fate . . .
But you, the sons of honor,
Companions of enjoyment,
Of love and poetry,
Carefree in all your pleasures,
Philosophers of leisure,
Who scorn the society
Of court slaves, come, dear comrades,
Come at a carefree moment,
Visit my little house—
To argue and carouse!
Lay down your load of sorrows,
Zhukovsky, my good friend!
Time flies by like an arrow,
Stealing our revelry.
Allow a friend to comfort
Your bitter woes, your tears,
And let Love reawaken
Enjoyment's withered rose!
Vyazemsky, scatter flowers
On your friends' troubled brows,
Pour out the foaming goblets

That Bacchus fills for us!
The Muses' true disciple,
Grandson of Aristippus,
You love a tender song,
The glasses' clash and clang.
In the refreshing coolness
Of suppers at your place
You love it when some beauty
Shoots you a tender glance.
You would abandon gladly
Fame and its sad cohort
Of noise and frantic folly
For just one moment's sport.
Friend of my idle moments,
Give me your hand once more,
And let us drown old tedium
In a golden goblet's foam!
While after us he chases,
The gray-haired god of time,
And strips the flowery meadows
With his unyielding scythe,
My friend, let's boldly venture
In search of happiness,
Drinking our fill of pleasure
Before the hour of death,
Secretly plucking flowers
From under time's sharp knife,
And spinning out the hours
Of our short-lasting life!
And when the gaunt-faced Parcae
Cut off that life's short thread,
And carry us to our fathers

In the night of the dead,
Then, my beloved comrades,
Do not bewail our fate!
What use are tears and sobbing
Or mercenary chants?
What use the smoking incense
Or the bells' dismal sound?
What use the mournful music
When we lie in the tomb?
What use . . . ? But then together
Under the moon's bright beams,
Come all, and scatter flowers
Where our dust lies in peace;
Or lay upon our tombstones
Figures of household gods,
A pair of flutes, two goblets,
Shoots of convolvulus,
And with no gilt inscription
The traveller will guess
That here those young companions
Are dust of happiness!

(Essays, 260–69)

The poem enjoyed immediate success and was much imitated, its form providing a model followed by many others. One of these, the schoolboy Pushkin, echoed the sentiments, the tone, and the form of "My Penates" very effectively in one of his first published poems, "The Little Town" (1815), accompanying it with an epistle to Batyushkov (in the same meter) wittily declining to follow the older poet's advice that he should write more serious poetry.

Eventually, at the beginning of the fateful year 1812, Batyushkov was able to heed the call of Gnedich and move to St. Petersburg in hope of government service. He was followed by the mocking letters of the young Vyazemsky, who poured scorn on the literary circles of the capital, notably on the Shishkov camp whose Circle (*beseda*, literally, "conversation") of Lovers of the Russian Word had its headquarters there. Batyushkov was happy enough to join in the mockery, replying: "I have to admit, dear friend, that our Petersburg originals tend to be even funnier than the Moscow ones. You can't imagine what goes on in the *Beseda*! What ignorance, what shamelessness!" He was particularly outraged by their criticism and mockery of Karamzin, "the only writer that the fatherland can take pride in" (*SPP*, 257). But against this ignorance he found allies in a group of clever young writers, including Dmitry Dashkov, a connoisseur of French literature and sharp-witted critic, to whom he was shortly to address one of his most important poems. Batyushkov joined in Dashkov's scandalous abuse of the ungifted writer Khvostov (see the end of the epistle to Zhukovsky given below), and when Dashkov was expelled from the *Beseda*, Batyushkov left with him (for which Vyazemsky unexpectedly scolded him).

All this was trivial literary politics, but eventually, thanks to Olenin's protection, Batyushkov obtained a government post (verging on a sinecure) as assistant keeper of manuscripts in the Imperial Library. Here he worked with Gnedich, Dashkov, and Krylov—congenial company indeed. This same period saw the beginning of his lasting love for Anna Furman, a poor and beautiful young woman who had been taken in by the Olenin family and with whom Gnedich had been in love three years earlier. She was never to respond fully to Batyushkov's love, but he carried her image in his heart when he went off to the wars, and once he was back, his feelings for her seem to have dominated his life for a number of years (see chapter 5).

In the meantime, Russia was plunged in war. On June 12, Napoleon took the fateful step of advancing into Russian territory, and a month later the Russian army was driven back from Smolensk to Moscow.

Vyazemsky, like many others, immediately went off to fight and took part in the battle of Borodino. But the frustrated Batyushkov was unable to join the army, being kept in bed for a month by a dangerous fever. It was from his sickroom that he wrote one more epistle to Zhukovsky, in the style and meter of "My Penates"—an apology for not visiting Moscow or the older poet's estate at Belyovo, a last Epicurean vision of happy country life, and a rueful self-portrait of the poet as sick man, finishing with unrepentant mockery of the hapless Khvostov (here called Svistov)—who may well have had the pleasure of reading it a couple of years later:

TO ZHUKOVSKY

Sorry, old balladeer,
Quiet hermit of Belyovo,
Phoebus be with you there,
He who was our protector!
In your humble country place
Deep in the fields, you're happy.
Like the young nightingale
In the dark wood's cool shadow,
Who gives his days to love,
From his nest never straying,
And all invisible sings,
Invisibly enthralling
The merry shepherd boys
And all the country people—
So you, with your sweet voice,
Among the humble pleasures
Of your enchanted home,
Sing your entrancing hymns.
O sing, good fortune's darling,

While Venus from above
Pours days of merrymaking
And the delights of love,
While golden luxury
And generosity
From their abundant treasure,
Serve you the choicest wines
And tumblers of fine porter
And juicy oranges
And truffle-scented pies—
All the old horn of plenty
That never will run dry—
To swell your succulent feast.
But look at me—the contrast!
Just see how the relentless
Small-town Hippocrates
In league with the pale fates
And hand in glove with the priests,
Brother of death and plague,
Boasting his skill in Latin
And his long years of practice,
Treats me with wormwood potions
And soups made out of bone,
And with these clever notions
He'll see me dead and gone
And send me to write epistles
On the banks of the Cocytus.
Everything has betrayed me
That filled my heart with pleasure,
All vanished like a dream:
The joys of love, Apollo
And health's ethereal gleam!

Now I am like a shadow
That fills all hearts with fear,
Dry, pale as a dead body,
With feeble, shaking knees,
My back a bow bent double,
My eyes all dim and shrunken,
And all my face is furrowed
With lines of misery.
My strength has turned to jelly,
My valor is brought low.
Alas! old friend, even Lila
Can't recognize me now.
With a malicious expression
Just yesterday she said
(As once cunning old Satan
Said to your noble hero):
Peace to the dear departed!
Peace to the dear departed!
Is that the only penance
Fate has decreed for me
For all my past transgressions?
No, there are newfound torments
In Satan's armory:
Here comes the dreaded Svistov
To read his compositions,
Bringing an idle singer,
A poor devil in tow,
Like him a tireless rhymer,
An oral killer too!
They keep on singing, chanting
All night, not drawing breath,
They keep on reading, reading—

> Exterminating angels,
>
> They'll read me to my death!

(Essays, 275–77)

Before long, however, Batyushkov had recovered and was once again involved in war and the consequences of war. From now on, the playful familiar epistle would give way to more direct and serious expressions of personal feeling that fall into the capacious genre of *elegy*.

04

BACK TO WAR

I n March 1813, nine months after his sickbed poem to Zhukovsky, Batyushkov wrote a quite different epistle. Addressed to his young literary friend Dmitry Dashkov, it marks a turning point in his work. It deals with a subject— war—which in the traditional poetics would have been treated in a high formal ode; Batyushkov's treatment shows his innovative genius, breaking down the barriers between genres, mixing different styles, solemn, lyrical, and familiar, to express an individual take on life. It is written in the short lines he favored for epistles, but in this poem we have the iambic tetrameters characteristic of eighteenth-century odes, as against the lighter trimeters of "My Penates":

TO DASHKOV

My friend, I've seen a sea of evil,
The punishments of vengeful heaven,
The fury of our enemies,
War and its devastating fires.
And I have seen the rich, the crowds
Of fugitives in tattered clothes,
And poor mothers pale as shrouds

Driven from their cherished homes.
At the crossroads I have seen them
Clutching their babies to the breast;
Bitterly I saw them weeping
And staring at the flaming red
Of the dark sky with a new shudder.
Three times since, aghast with horror,
I've walked through devastated Moscow
Among the ruins and the graves;
Three times since, my tears of sorrow
Have watered the city's sacred ash.
There, in the streets, where mighty buildings,
The ancient towers of the tsars,
Were witnesses of former glories
And of the fame of later years;
There where the holy monks of old
Now rest in peace through passing time,
And as the centuries unfold,
Nothing disturbs their sacred shrines;
There where in days of peaceful labor
The hand of luxury had made
Among the golden domes of Moscow
Gardens and parks—now all I met
Was embers, ashes, piles of stone,
Bodies heaped high along the river,
And pallid regiments of soldiers
Wandering through the ruined town! . . .
And you, my friend, you, my dear comrade,
Want me to sing of love and joy,
Of carefree happiness and leisure,
Of wine and youthful revelry!
And in the city's dreadful glare

Among the fearful storms of war,
To call the nymphs and shepherds here
With carols to the dancing floor!
To sing of the sweet blandishments
Of Armidas and fickle Circes
Among the graves of my dear friends
Fallen on the field of glory!
No, no! let my talent waste away
And let the lyre, so dear to friendship,
Perish if ever I forget
Moscow the golden, my dear homeland!
No, no! until the day I bring
My life, the love of my own country
As a sacrifice fit to avenge
The honor of my fathers' city;
Until with that hero whose wounds
Led him along the path to glory[1]
I have three times taken my stand
Against the ranks of hostile warriors;
My friend, until that blessed time
I shall not know muses or graces,
Love and its passionate embraces,
Or the tumultuous joys of wine!

(Essays, 237–39)

This poem quickly became regarded as the most significant poetic reaction to the destruction of Moscow in 1812. We don't know what suggestion from Dashkov prompted such an outburst of feeling, but the grief and patriotic fervor expressed here were real enough. Batyushkov had indeed been three times through the "sacred ashes" of Moscow, and was able to write realistic descriptions of the French invasion and the great fire that destroyed the city in 1812. A letter to

Gnedich after his first visit in October 1812 reads like a prose draft for the poem:

> From Tver to Moscow and from Moscow to Nizhny Novgorod I saw, I saw whole families of all conditions and all ages in the most pitiful situation; I saw what I had not seen in Prussia or in Sweden: whole provinces forced to move! I saw poverty, despair, fires, hunger and all the horrors of war, and I shuddered as I looked at the earth, the heavens and myself.
>
> *(SP, 335)*

Batyushkov stood out among his contemporaries for his refusal of both frivolous indifference and false heroics. From the beginning of the invasion, he had understood the dangers of the situation, but at the same time, he would always reject the patriotic embellishment of feats of arms.

For months, though, he was unable to participate in the fight against Napoleon. Illness and shortage of money prevented him from joining his friend Vyazemsky for the battle of Borodino, fought in early September (late August according to the Russian calendar). Just a few days before Borodino he had been called to Moscow to look after Mikhail Muravyov's widow, Ekaterina Fyodorovna, who was ill, isolated, and living in a *dacha* outside the city, with the French troops approaching. While he was there, he received a letter from his friend Petin, written just before Borodino. The letter made a deep impression, as he later recalled in his "Memories of Petin": "We were in a terrible panic in Moscow, and I was amazed at the mental calm emanating from every line of a letter scribbled down on a drum at a fateful moment." This businesslike tranquility, allied to Petin's desire to fight for his country, a desire free of all hatred—all this aroused Batyushkov's envy: "Fortunate friend, you shed your blood on the field of Borodino, the field of honor, within sight of your beloved Moscow, and I could not share this honor with you!" (*Essays*, 404). Instead, his role was to escort Ekaterina Fyodorovna to Nizhny Novgorod, two hundred miles to the east, where Moscow society had taken refuge.

In Nizhny, the refugees amused themselves as best they could, re-creating some of the "balls, charades, and masquerades" of Moscow, but Batyushkov found it hard to take part in this. In the letter to Gnedich just quoted, he continues: "The dreadful acts of the Vandals, i.e. the French, in and around Moscow, acts without precedent in history, have utterly upset my little philosophy and turned me against the human race" (*SP*, 335). And in a letter to Vyazemsky, he described the doings of the French invaders as "the fruits of enlightenment, or rather of vice, in that wittiest of nations which could pride itself on Henri IV and Fénelon" (*SPP*, 383). Vyazemsky advised him against joining the army, but Batyushkov had made up his mind to do what "duty, reason and the heart" demanded. He persuaded General Bakhmetev to take him on as an adjutant, but he still had to wait more than six months. In this time, he traveled to and fro between Nizhny and Vologda, passing through the ruins of Moscow, then in February 1813 returned to St. Petersburg, where he was reunited with his literary friends. It was these meetings and conversations that sparked the epistle to Dashkov.

While he awaited the long-delayed call to arms, the Russian troops had crossed the Niemen and were pursuing the French through Poland and Prussia. Batyushkov, meanwhile, was filling his time with literary battles, directing more satire against familiar targets. With a friend, he produced a sequel to the "Vision on the Banks of Lethe," entitled "A Bard at the Circle of Lovers of the Russian Word." Parodying Zhukovsky's patriotic "A Bard in the Camp of Russian Warriors," it figures an enthusiastic poet leading the band of Archaists in a ritual of self-glorification. Shishkov, who by this time was serving in the army, reappears in all his glory:

> All honor to you, Slavenophile,
>   Indomitable champion!
> You have put paid to reason's rule,
>   Untiring in your chanting.

(Essays, 369)

This was just a squib (later described by its author as "a very silly joke"), but like the "Vision," it circulated widely in manuscript copies, being printed much later. It foreshadows the satirical games of the Arzamas group that Batyushkov joined a couple of years later.

At more or less the same time as this poem and the epistle to Dashkov, he was practicing his German by translating some of Schiller's *The Bride of Messina* (*Die Braut von Messina*), but also trying his hand at war poetry. The romance "Parting" sets out to be a worldly-wise soldier's poem, inspired by the "hussar" verse of Denis Davydov; it soon became a popular song. In this piece it seems as if Batyushkov is deliberately avoiding a serious view of war and of love:

PARTING

> Propped on his saber, there he stood,
> The hussar, plunged in woe;
> Leaving his girl for years, he sighed
> As he prepared to go:
>
> "Don't cry, my pretty one! No tears
> Can ward off evil days.
> By my honor and moustache, I swear
> My love I'll not betray!

Love's an unconquerable force!
It shields me in the war;
With a true heart and a good sword
What danger can I fear?

Don't cry, my pretty one! No tears
Can ward off evil days.
If I betray our love . . . I swear
By my moustache I'll pay!

Then let him stumble, my good steed,
As I ride to the fight,
And let my soldier's bridle snap
And the stirrups at my feet!

Let my good sword shatter in my hand
And break like rotten wood,
And me, all pale and trembling, stand
Where once before I stood!"

But his good steed did not stumble there
Beneath our gallant soldier;
His sword was still unshattered there—
And with it his hussar's honor!

But he forgot the love and tears
Of his dear shepherdess,
On a foreign soil plucked happiness
With another lovely lass.

And the shepherdess, what did she do?
Gave her heart to another.

For lovely girls love is a toy,
Their promises—just blather!

True love, my friends, has flown away,
And cheating rules the land,
While laughing Cupid writes our oaths
With his arrow in the sand.

(Essays, 292–93)

The second of these war poems is of a quite different kind. On the first day of 1813, the Russian army had crossed the river Niemen (Neman), driving the French forces back to the west. Batyushkov was not present, but he used eyewitness accounts to paint a picture of the crossing in which realistic images mingle with a more traditional eloquence. Only a fragment remains of what was to have been a much longer poem:

RUSSIAN TROOPS CROSSING THE NEMAN
ON THE FIRST OF JANUARY 1813

The somber Neman was sleeping wrapped in snow.
The plain of icy waves, the empty shore,
The villages abandoned by the river,
     All were lit up by the dim moon.
All empty . . . dark upon the snow in places
Corpses are lying, a campfire smokes and dwindles
     And, cold as a dead man,
     A fugitive sits and thinks
     There in the road, alone,
His eyes fixed, dull, unmoving, on his deadened feet.
On all sides silence . . . And see, in the empty distance,

A forest of massed spears has sprung from the earth!
It moves. The shields and swords and armor resonate
And menacingly in the somber night
The banners, horses, warriors all show black:
The regiments of Slavs carrying death
Pursue the foe, they reach the river, ground their spears,
And from the snow unnumbered tents have risen
      And campfires burning on the shore
Have curtained all the sky in a red glow.
      In the camp the young emperor
      Sits among his generals,
By him an ancient leader, gleaming gray,
      In the martial beauty of age.

                                     (*Essays*, 343)

The "young emperor" is Tsar Alexander I, whom Batyushkov was to see (and admire) for the first time later in the same year, since eventually, in July, he was allowed to leave St. Petersburg and head west.

Traveling by way of Vilnius and Warsaw, he joined the Russian army in Prague. Here he was attached as adjutant to the war-hardened General Nikolay Raevsky, who was later to befriend the young Pushkin during his southern exile. Batyushkov admired Raevsky intensely; he helped to care for him when he was seriously wounded, and they spent several months at close quarters. His admiration stopped short of idolatry, however, and his reports of conversations with the general helped to dispel a "noble Roman" legend that had gathered around him (see *Essays*, 412–16); here again, he anticipates the Tolstoy of *War and Peace*, who has his hero Nikolay Rostov cast doubt on the same legend.[2]

Batyushkov was soon in action, going under fire in the battle of Kulm. Here he was reunited with his old friend Ivan Petin, now a youthful colonel; a sketch of 1815–1816 entitled "Memory of Places, Battles and Travels" gives a vivid, if rather literary, account of their conversations during a pause in the hostilities:

> The whole camp rises up in my imagination, and thousands of trivial details enliven this imagination. My heart drowns in pleasure: I am sitting in my friend Petin's hut at the foot of a high mountain crowned with the ruins of a feudal castle. We are alone. We talk openly, from the heart; we cannot see enough of one another after our long separation. The danger from which we had emerged unscathed, the noise, movement and activity of army life, the sight of the troops and their ammunition, the simple military hospitality of a friend, a comrade of my youth, a bottle of Bohemian wine resting on a drum, a handful of fruit and a piece of stale bread, *parca mensa*, a simple meal, but lovingly prepared—all this combined to make us happy as children.
>
> (*Essays, 396–97*)

Before long the two friends were involved in an even more bloody conflict, the battle of Leipzig, which made a deep impression on Batyushkov. On the first day of the battle Raevsky was badly wounded and had to be helped from the field. Then Petin was killed in action and buried in a makeshift grave. In his "Memories of Petin," Batyushkov writes:

> I saw this grave, covered with fresh earth; I stood over it in deep sorrow and gave relief to my heart with tears. It contained the most precious treasure of my life—friendship. I asked, begged the respectable and very ancient priest of the village to preserve the fragile memorial, a simple wooden cross, with the brave young man's name inscribed on it.
>
> (*Essays, 408*)

The scene recurs in one of Batyushkov's greatest poems, the elegy "Shade of a Friend." Batyushkov himself came very near to being taken prisoner; as an adjutant, he was sent by the general to carry messages, and described what he experienced in a letter to Gnedich:

> On the 7th [of September, Russian style], the general sent me early in the morning to Bernadotte's army to inquire about his son. I rode all round Leipzig and saw all the horrors of war. The battlefield was still fresh—and what a field it was! For most of ten miles, there were piles of human bodies at every step, together with dead horses and shattered shell-cases and gun-carriages. Heaps of shells and the moans of the dying.
>
> (SP, 343)

He concludes with a French tag from La Fontaine: *ce sont là jeux de princes* (such is the sport of princes).

Leipzig was Batyushkov's cruelest exposure to the horrors of war. Thereafter he accompanied Raevsky to convalesce in Weimar, finding it dull and disagreeable, even if it was Goethe's city. His soldier's view of the place is spelled out in another letter to Gnedich:

> We've been in Weimar ten days or so now; we lead a quiet, boring life. There is no society. The Germans are fond of the Russians, all except my landlord, who poisons me daily with filthy soup and baked apples. There's nothing to be done about this; neither I nor my comrades have a pfennig until we get our pay. I wander around like a Scythian in the land of Goethe, Wieland and other learned folk. Occasionally I go to the theatre. The auditorium is not bad, but poorly lit. They play comedies, dramas, operas and tragedies—the last of these rather well, to my surprise. I liked *Don Carlos* greatly and am reconciled to Schiller.
>
> (SP, 345)

Two months later the army moved through a series of German cities toward France, crossing the frontier into Alsace on the last day of 1813. This frontier was the Rhine, and Batyushkov later made this crossing the subject of one of the monumental "historical elegies" he wrote in 1816–1817, comparable in its ambition to "Tasso Dying." There are realistic elements here, as in all of Batyushkov's war writings, but the picture is heightened and idealized, with a courtier-like reference in the tenth stanza to "Russia's benediction" (Tsar Alexander's wife, who was born on the banks of the Rhine). Aiming at a kind of epic grandeur that he had not previously attempted in poetry, Batyushkov sets the current moment and his individual experience in a vast historical context, from the Roman legions to the invasion of Napoleon, culminating in the arrival of the Russian liberators:

THE CROSSING OF THE RHINE—1814

The troops come riding through the fields. My horse
Rejoices when he sees your waters gleaming
    Far off, O Rhine, and whinnies,
Breaks from the ranks and gallops to the shore
      Borne up on wings of thirst;
      Then gulps your icy flood,
      Bathing his weary chest
      In your life-giving cold.

O precious day! I am standing by the Rhine!
I gaze with greedy eyes down from the hills
    And greet the mountains, fields
And feudal castles wrapped in cloud and rain,
      And the land rich in fame
      And ancient memory

Where from the Alps eternally
You pour your mighty waves.

Witness of ancient days, of centuries,
O Rhine, those countless legions drank from you
    Who with their swords wrote laws
For the proud wandering tribes of Germany.
        Fate's darling, freedom's scourge,
        Here Caesar fought and won,
        And his steed swam across
        Your sacred waters, Rhine!

Centuries passed; the cross now ruled your waves,
And love and honor filled men's souls and thoughts;
    Knights took up arms and fought
To save fair ladies' honor, orphans' lives.
        Here in their tournaments
        The champions' sharp swords rang;
        Here even today we sense
        The troubadours' sweet song.

And here, beneath the shade of oak and fig,
In the sweet murmur of the mountain streams,
    In happy villages and towns
Passion still lives among the chosen few.
        Here inspiration flows
        From old simplicities,
        The sacred love of home
        And scorn for luxuries.

Everything here, the fields, the sacred waters,
Which knew time's mysteries, the voice of bards,

Everything gives new power
To lofty feelings and high-flying thoughts.
Free, proud, half-savage, once
True priests of nature sang
The old Germanic songs . . .
But their spellbinding choirs are gone.

And you, great river, witness of all time,
You, still today so calm, so regal,
With your proud nation's fall
You too have bowed your head in captive shame.
How long now have you flowed
In sorrow past the hordes
Of hostile troops who bear
The new Attila's eagles?

How long is it since those who till your banks
Among their ancient vineyards first encountered
The alien regiments
And met the hostile gaze of foreign soldiers?
How long have they been drinking
Your wine in crystal cups,
And sending horses trampling
Your fields and your ripe crops?

The hour has struck! We sons of the north have come
Under our Moscow flag with fire and freedom;
We come from icy seas,
From the warm breakers of the Caspian,
From far-away Baikal,
From Dnieper, Don and Volga,
From Peter's granite walls,

From Caucasus and Ural.

We have come in thunder to defend your name,
The honor of your arms, your wasted fields,
     Your villages, the sacred place
Where Russia's benediction bloomed in peace;
     The land of the bright angel
     Born for the midnight lands
     And given by Providence
     To tsar and grateful Russia.

We are here, O Rhine, you see our biting swords!
You hear the noise of troops, the neighing horses,
     Hurrahs of victory and shouts
Of heroes galloping down to your wide waters.
     Sending dust flying,
     Trampling the enemy dead,
     The horses soon are drinking,
     Crowded on the soft earth.

What a rich feast for eyes and ears! We see
The horses, then the gleam of the bronze cannons,
     The muskets ranged in battle,
And ancient flags among the shields and spears;
     The plumes of soldiers' helmets,
     The ranks of heavy horses,
     And the light cavalry—
     Reflected in the water!

We hear the axes ring, the forest felled!
The campfires smoke and flare above the Rhine;
     The festive goblets clink,

The soldiers' joyful shouts rise to the skies;
    A warrior hugs his friend,
    Another whets his bayonet,
    A horseman with a threatening hand
    Brandishes a winged dart.

And there a rider, leaning on his spear,
Alone and pensive, stands on the high bank
    And with an eager eye
Follows the river's winding course. Perhaps
    His memory is recalling
    The river of his homeland,
    And to his breast, unthinking,
    He presses his bronze cross.

But over here a bloodless sacrifice
Is ordered by the generals among the heaps
    Of trophies, and the priest
Kneels here before the God of the Maccabees.
    Above him rustles and waves
    The forest of our banners;
    The young sun in the heavens
    Makes our high altar blaze.

The cries of war fall silent; in the ranks
Devotion suddenly seals the soldiers lips;
    The weapons are all dipped
Leaders and warriors bow their heads in thanks.
    Then to our God they sing,
    To you, the Lord of Hosts,
    You never-failing sun,

The peaceful offerings smoke.

Now they all move away, line after line;
Like a great sea the army moves and flows,
  And a heroic cry
Never yet heard by you, O Rhine, resounds;
  Your welcoming shores give voice,
  The bridge trembles at our shouts;
  The enemy, seeing us, flees
  And vanishes from sight.

(*Essays, 320–24*)

Battles, marches, and countermarches brought the Russian army
to the gates of Paris. On the way, however, Batyushkov had taken
time out to visit Cirey, the country mansion where Voltaire had
lived with his lover, the physicist and mathematician Madame du
Châtelet. He subsequently wrote about this visit in an open letter to
Dashkov, published in 1816 under the title "A Journey to the Château
de Cirey"; this is partly a tourist's report, partly an homage to two
remarkable people—though it is interesting to see that the fulsome
praise of Voltaire is largely attributed to the writer's companion. It is
a romantically nostalgic visit: as the travelers approach Cirey, they
meet an old man in a worn-out revolutionary cap, who tells them:
"Time and revolution have destroyed everything. . . . They planted a
tree of liberty. . . . They destroyed God's churches. . . . And how did
it all finish? The tree has been chopped down and the inscription on
the church porch, *Liberty, fraternity, or death*, has been whitewashed
over" (*Essays*, 105–6). A long note points up the contrast between
the Germans, who love and preserve the past, and the French, for
whom nothing is sacred. France, once so much admired, no lon-
ger offers a model of civilization. In Voltaire's study the Russians

declaim the odes of Derzhavin and Lomonosov, and Batyushkov cites Voltaire's own words: "C'est du Nord à présent que nous vient la lumière" (It is from the North that the light shines today). Russia is the victorious power (*Essays*, 111–12).

Then on March 16–18 came the triumphal entry into Paris. A few days later, Batyushkov wrote again to Gnedich: "From the heights of Montreuil I saw Paris, wrapped in thick mist, an endless row of houses dominated by the lofty towers of Notre Dame. I confess my heart began to beat with joy!" (*SP*, 354). There was no fighting, and the Russian troops marched into the city to the hurrahs of the Parisians. In a letter to Zhukovsky some months later, Batyushkov described this as a "marvelous moment, worth a whole life" (*SP*, 379). He spent two months in Paris, looking at all the sights, visiting the opera, drinking in celebrated coffee houses and restaurants, and even attending a session of the French Academy. He was not greatly impressed by this sanctuary of French literature, and commented: "In the usual way of things, I think the age of glory for French literature has gone and is unlikely ever to return" (*SP*, 365). This remark comes from a rather literary letter addressed to Dashkov, one of the very few accounts he left of his time in Paris. He says little of the riches of the art galleries for fear of boring his correspondent, but he does allow himself some admiring words for Parisian women and their feet:

> For them love pours out
> All his golden arrows.
> All is enchanting,
> Their walk, their light figure,
> Their arms, half-bared,
> Their eyes full of pleasure,
> Magic sounds on their lips
> And passionate words.

Everything charms you—
And, dear friends . . . their feet!
The Graces' creation,
Companions of Venus;
For such feet gods eternal
Spread the way with roses
Or smooth it with swan's down.
Phidias before them
Would drown in emotion;
The poet is in heaven,
And the penitent, weeping,
Abandons his prayers.

(CP, 169–70)

The stay in Paris was pleasant enough, but after the initial rapture, Batyushkov was not bowled over. He has severe things to say on the old topics of French frivolity and the fickle affections of the Paris crowd. By the middle of May, having fallen ill, he is writing to Vyazemsky of his pleasure in imagining his return to Moscow and his friends: "I entered Paris full of enthusiasm and I am leaving it with joy" (*SPP*, 277). In "The Prisoner," possibly written in France, but more likely after his return to Russia, he gives a sympathetic depiction of the very Russian nostalgia of Lev Davydov, brother of the poet, who was a prisoner of war in France. Here is a stanza "sung" by the captive:

Sound sweetly, sound, waves of the Rhone,
    Water the golden fields,
But let the voice of my own Don
    Sound through your song to me!
O winds, sweep down through the dark night
    From the land I call my own,

> And you, stars of the North, burn bright
> On one so far from home!

(Essays, 244)

Not being a prisoner, Batyshkov no doubt felt less longing for home than his lyrical hero, but he neglected the opportunity to see more of France, and on May 17 set off on his return journey. He did not go by the direct overland route, but took advantage of an invitation from a friend, Dmitry Severin, who was on a diplomatic mission to London, and returned to St. Petersburg by sea, with brief stays in England and Sweden. It seems to have been his first experience of sea travel.

Unfortunately, we know little about his time in England. He arrived in London at a propitious moment, shortly after the tumultuous reception given to the tsar and the Don Cossack leader Platov, and he seems to have been surrounded by good friends from the Russian embassy. In a letter written to Severin in mid-June, after he had reached Sweden, he is lyrical in his praise of British life and society:

> So, my friend, the land in which everything flourishes, a land piled high, so to speak, with the riches of the whole world, can only sustain itself by its unfailing respect for social and divine manners and laws.
>
> These are the foundations for the freedom and prosperity of the new Carthage, that wonderful island where luxury and simplicity, the power of the king and of the citizen are constantly set against one another in a perfect equilibrium. This mixture of luxury and simplicity is what impressed me most in the homeland of Elizabeth and Addison.

(SP, 369–70)

This ideal view of Britain owes something to Voltaire's *English Letters* and might not have survived a longer residence. But Batyushkov was in London for only a couple of weeks before setting off for home. He sailed from Harwich, where he was kept waiting by contrary winds. This gave him time to visit a church, where the "simplicity of the service," the music, the angelic faces of the women, the numerous children, and the sailors' weather-beaten faces left a "deep and delightful impression" on him. Once he was on board, he had to put up with seasickness and with some tedious fellow travelers, but he enjoyed the poetry of sea travel. He wrote to Severin:

> I spent my free hours on deck in a sweet enchantment, reading Homer and Tasso, the soldier's true companions. Often, setting my book aside, I gazed with admiration on the open sea. How marvelous are those boundless, endless waves! What an inexpressible feeling was born in the depths of my soul! How freely I breathed! How my eyes and my imagination flew from one side of the horizon to the other!
>
> *(SP, 372)*

A nocturnal version of this enchantment is the setting for one of Batyushkov's most moving poems, an elegy for his lost friend Ivan Petin, the noble victim of the Napoleonic wars:

SHADE OF A FRIEND

Sunt aliquid manes: letum non omnia finit
Luridaque evictos effugit umbra rogos

(Propertius)

    I sailed from the misty shores of Albion;
Beneath the leaden waves I seemed to see them sink.

In the ship's wake fluttered the halcyon
And with its quiet singing cheered the sailors' work.
  The evening breeze, the billows' buffeting,
The same unchanging noise, the beating of the sails,
  And on the deck the helmsman's cry
To the lookout who dreamed above the murmuring waves,
  All these were food for my sweet reverie.
As if in an enchantment I stood by the mast,
  And through the misty air and the gray night
My eyes were seeking my beloved Northern Star.
  My thoughts were all engulfed in memory
Of my dear native land and of my native sky.
  But the wind's music and the rocking sea
Weighed on my eyes with languorous oblivion,
  And dream succeeded dream
And suddenly . . . was I asleep? . . . I saw the friend
  Who perished in the fateful fight
And by the Pleisse's waters met his noble end.
  But the sight brought no fear; his brow
  Preserved no trace of his deep wounds,
And like an April morning shone with joy,
Bringing the light of heaven to my mind.
"My dear friend, is it you, comrade of my best days?
Can it be you?—I cried—ever beloved warrior!
Did I not weep at your untimely burial,
Lit by the fearful glare of martial flames,
  Did I not with true friends inscribe
Your valor with the sword's edge on the wood,
Accompanying your soul to its celestial home
  With groans and prayers and tears?
Shade of the unforgotten, dear friend, speak!
Or was the past all only a mirage, a dream,

All, the pale corpse, the grave, the solemn rite
Performed by friendship to your memory?
O, say one word to me! Let that familiar sound
    Once more caress my eager ear,
And let me, o my unforgotten friend,
    Press your hand lovingly in mine! . . ."
And I flew to him . . . But the ethereal shade
Vanished in the blue depths of cloudless sky
Like smoke, a meteor, or a nightmare vision,
    And sleep fell from my eyes.

Beneath the canopy of silence all was sleeping;
The fearful elements seemed to make no noise.
From a thin veil of cloud the moon shone down,
The waves lay dark, the breeze was barely stirring,
But sweet tranquility had gone from me,
    My soul flew where the shade had fled,
Still longing to detain its heavenly guest—
You, my dear brother, my beloved friend!

                          (Essays, 222–23)

The Latin epigraph is the opening of Propertius's Elegy IV.7: "The spirits of the dead are something real: death does not end everything, and the pale shade flies from the quenched pyre." In the Latin poem, the poet dreams of his dead lover Cynthia, who comes to taunt him with his cowardice and other faults; in the end, the shade slips from his grasp and vanishes. Batyushkov's poem, while also suspended between the appearance and disappearance of a "shade," is quite different in tone, with none of Propertius's bitter cynicism; it is closer to the meetings with the spirits of the dead that one finds in Virgil's *Aeneid*, especially Aeneas's vision of his wife Creusa at the end of book 2. But in any case, the poem echoes the world of

Latin poetry that Batyushkov had learned to love in the society of
Muravyov and Olenin, now given a worthy subject by the experi-
ence of war. The style is nobly serious throughout, moving from the
dreamlike vision of a sea voyage to the dramatic confrontation with
the shade and back again, but always maintaining the harmony that
contemporaries so admired in his poetry. Some years later, Pushkin
wrote of "Shade of a Friend": "Beauty, perfection—what harmony!"

The soldier carries with him Homer and Tasso, and quotes from
Propertius, but there is one other classical poet who was perhaps
even closer to him: Tibullus. Batyushkov was known to some as the
"Russian Parny" or the "Russian Tasso," but he also called himself a
"little Tibullus." He had begun translating extracts from the elegies
in 1809, using French translations as well as the original Latin. Some
time in 1814, however, he produced a very free translation of the
whole of Elegy III.1, a poem addressed to the Roman poet's patron
Messala. With its painful image of war and its longing for Delia, this
poem must have struck a chord in Batyushkov, giving rise to a beau-
tiful Russian elegy, which stands well alone. The opening section
complains of the poet's loneliness, far from both his patron and his
beloved. This leads into a development on the golden age, where
Batyushkov's familiar household gods come into their own:

> Dear Goddess, give me back the fields of home,
> The old familiar murmur of the stream,
> And give me Delia! I will bring you gifts,
> O Lares and Penates, bring rich offerings.
> Why do we not live still in the Golden Age?
> The tribes of people in those carefree days
> Had not yet driven roads through hills and forests,
> And not yet torn the earth apart with ploughshares;
> No pine or spruce yet flew with light-winged sails,
> Chased by the wind, across the azure seas,

No helmsman would have dared to make his way
In a frail vessel over the furious waves;
The sturdy oxen wandered through the meadow
Trampling the sweet grass, sleeping in green shadow,
The swift steed never stained the bit with blood;
No boundary post, no columns marred the land,
The village doors stood open to the wind;
Honey dripped from the oaks in amber streams,
And from the udders of the grazing sheep
Milk poured abundantly into the bowls.
O peaceful shepherds who, with guiltless souls,
Lived without care in the dumb wilderness!
In your time no one brought unhappiness
To friends by hammering sharp-bladed swords,
And in the fields no clash of arms was heard.
O Age of Jupiter! Miserable days!
War everywhere, and hunger and disease,
Death on all sides, on water and on land . . .
But you, who hold the thunder in your hand,
Look graciously on me, your peaceful poet!
I never broke the faith in word or thought,
Tremblingly I adored the godly band,
And if fate brings me an untimely end,
May a stone tell the passerby of me:
"Tibullus, Messala's friend, lies here in peace."
My only god, master of every heart,
Dear son of Venus, here I was your bard.
I have worn your tender fetters all my life,
And you, Amor, will bear me secretly
Into Elysium, and the meadows there
Where an eternal May-time haunts the air,
Heavy with spikenard and cinnamon

And fragrant with sweet musk roses in bloom;
There we shall hear the birds', the waters' voice,
There the young maidens in their choral dance
Move through the woods like fleeting apparitions,
And he who is struck down, caught in the passion
Of love's embraces, he whom fate lays low,
Wears a fresh sprig of myrtle on his brow . . .

A twenty-line passage on the contrasting fate of the damned then leads into a final section addressed directly to the poet's beloved; one can imagine that the name Delia here hides a dream of an idealized Anna Furman, the girl he had left behind in St. Petersburg:

May he who broke our peace and parted us
Suffer the torments of deep Tartarus!
But you, so true to me, my precious friend,
Even in a quiet hut where none can find
You and your soul mate, she who knows your passion,
Don't leave the household altars for a moment.
When winter blizzards howl, in this safe shelter
Your friend in the dark night will light a candle
And, turning the distaff softly in her palm,
Will tell you stories of your mother's time,
And you, lending an ear to these old tales,
Will nod, my love, and sleep will close your eyes,
And quietly from your lap the spinning wheel
Will fall. . . . And at the door I shall appear
Like a good angel suddenly sent from heaven.
Run then to greet me, out from your peaceful haven,
In lovely nakedness appear to me,
Your hair spread on your shoulders carelessly,
Your lily-white breast and your lovely feet . . .

O when will Aurora with her rosy steeds,
Blazing with light, bring us that blessed day,
And rapt Tibullus embrace his Delia?

(Essays, 206–10)

This rendering of Tibullus was a primary inspiration for Osip Mandelstam's "Tristia," one of the great elegies of the twentieth century.

Batyushkov's journey brought the poet to Gothenburg, from where he moved on to Stockholm and then by way of Finland back home to St. Petersburg. His short stay in Sweden, though it was a disappointment after London, did spark in Batyushkov a romantic vision of the old Scandinavian world, comparable to that seen in the 1808 "Letters of a Russian Officer in Finland." This time it produced a full-scale poem, partly inspired by a considerably longer German poem by Friedrich von Matthison, "Elegy written in the ruins of an old castle" (Elegie in den Ruinen eines altes Bergschlosses geschrieben). Like the German poem, Batyushkov's elegy looks back to a vanished heroic past, though here it is not the poet's national past. Like the somewhat later "Crossing of the Rhine," it is written in an elevated style, with a formal pattern reminiscent of the solemn Russian odes of the eighteenth century and a distinctly Ossianic atmosphere:[3]

ON THE RUINS OF A CASTLE IN SWEDEN

The day's great eye is flaming in the west
    And gently sinking in the ocean
The moon peers pensively through a thin mist
    On shores and inlets lapped in silence.
The seas all round are plunged in a deep sleep;
Only from time to time fishermen calling
Send long-drawn voices echoing and resounding
    In the night's quiet lap.

Above the waves the lofty cliffs are dark
      Where in the sacred shade of oak trees
I wander deep in thought, seeking the marks
      Of years gone by and vanished glory:
Ruins, fierce ramparts, a moat full of grass,
Columns, a shaky bridge with chains of iron,
Moss-covered towers with battlements of granite,
      And a long row of graves.

Everything is asleep, and silence reigns,
      But memories are gently stirring;
The traveler leaning on a mossy grave
      Dreams sweetly, as he sees the ivy
That twists and climbs, clinging to the stone steps,
The shriveled wormwood that the wind caresses,
The moon that silvers over the grim fortress
      Above the somnolent deep.

Here once a fighting man of Odin's blood,
      Gray-headed after years of warfare,
Sent off his son to fight, with his scarred hand
      Giving the youth his feathered arrows,
His ancient armor and his heavy sword,
And loudly cried out, with his arms uplifted
"He is marked out for you, you god of battles,
      Always and everywhere!

And you, my son, swear by your father's sword,
      Swear with the solemn oath of Hela,
To be the terror of the western world
      Or like our ancients, perish bravely!"
And the bold youth kissed the ancestral blade

And pressed to his breast his father's gauntlet
Trembling with joy—so at the sound of conflict
 Trembles the eager steed.

War to the enemies of the fatherland!
 A clamor fills the port till morning,
The seas are foaming as on every hand
 The storm-winged ships fly from their mooring.
In Neustria the clash of arms is loud,
The whole of misty Albion is blazing,
And Hela night and day brings to Valhalla
 Pale legions of the dead.

Young man, make haste back to your native shores
 Carrying with you the spoils of battle!
A gentle breeze is breathing in your sails
 O hero, born to grace Valhalla!
High in the hills the scalds prepare a feast,
The oak trees blaze, and mead in goblets sparkles,
The herald of good news sings to the fathers
 Of victories overseas.

At golden dawn here in the port of peace
 Your bride-to-be awaits your coming;
She has been praying to the gods in tears
 To look with favor on your voyage.
And now, a fleet of swans, through misty veils
The ships glide through the waters, shining whitely;
Blow, following wind, and let your quiet stirring
 Swell all the vessels' sails.

The ship has docked, the hero brings with him

The spoils of war, the captive women;
His father greets him, and his youthful bride,
And the scalds glow with inspiration.
The beautiful young woman, silent, weeping,
Hardly dares raise her timid eyes and look
At her young hero, turning pale then blushing,
A moon among the clouds.

And where the gray stones in a mossy row
Mark how the graveyard lies in ruin,
And through the night from time to time an owl
Sends out a cry of desolation—
There joyful cups on festive tables rang,
There warriors met to feast in celebration,
There the scalds sang of warfare and their fingers
Flew over fiery strings.

They sang of the clash of swords, the arrows' flight,
The clang of shields, the din of battle,
Villages laid waste in the fierce fight,
And cities that the flames have gutted.
The elders listened greedily to their song,
Their brimming goblets shook between their fingers,
And their proud hearts exalted to remember
Their fame when they were young.

But now the place is wrapped in night's grim mist;
Time has turned everything to ashes!
Where once the scald shook music from the strings,
Only the dismal wind now whistles!
Where chieftains triumphed with their loyal men
And poured out wine to the great god of battle,

A pair of trembling deer sleep in the shelter
　　Until the new day dawns.

Where are you now, you giants of the north,
　　You who plunged Gaul in dark commotion,
Companions of Roald, who in your frail boats
　　Once sailed across the distant ocean?
Where are you, daring warriors of yore,
You, the wild sons of battle and of freedom,
Who grew amid the snows and native wildness
　　Amid the spears and swords?

The mighty men are gone! But not in vain
　　The traveler questions the dark boulders
And reads the secret runes, the dumb remains
　　Of ancient ways that time has crumbled.
The villager, leaning on his staff proclaims:
"Look on this place, you child of foreign peoples;
Here our forefathers' relics lie and molder:
　　Respect their resting place!"

　　　　　　　　　　　　　　　　(*Essays, 202–5*)

But as in Finland in 1809, Batyushkov was not the dupe of his own romantic vision of Scandinavia; if this world ever existed, it was gone forever now. Looking about him, he saw the rather different reality of modern Swedish society and wrote it down in a rueful little satire included in the letter to Severin from Gothenburg:

I'm in the land of mists and rains,
Where Scandinavians of old
Loved honor and their simple ways,
Wine and war and the clashing sword.

Leaving these lofty cliffs, these caves,
Scorning the deep ocean's waves,
In their frail boats they'd boldly steer
To strike their foes with awe and fear.
Here Odin received a fearful sacrifice.
Here altars were red with the blood of prisoners . . .
But a mighty transformation greets our eyes:
    Now these same northern tsars
Nibble their ginger cake and smoke tobacco,
    They read the *Gotha Echo*
And sit and yawn together at the stars.

(CP, 254–55)

The juxtaposition of these two Nordic poems points to a constant romantic tension in Batyushkov's writing. He dreamed of an idealized past, the glory of ancient Hellas, the Renaissance of Petrarch and Tasso, or the violent world of the sagas, but he had to live in a far from heroic present. Perhaps the Napoleonic wars gave him the chance to live a nobler, more active life, but once this episode was over, he had to settle to the frustrations of a rather impoverished civilian existence. His return to Russia was nevertheless to be a return to literary life and to poetry.

05

THE RETURN OF ODYSSEUS

In July 1814, Batyushkov finally arrived back in St. Petersburg, where he was to stay for the next few months. Some time that autumn he wrote a short poem, in fact a free translation of a poem by Schiller:

THE RETURN OF ODYSSEUS

The suffering, god-fearing Odysseus,
Seeking his Ithaca, was doomed to wander
Among the terrors of the earth and seas;
With a bold tread he trespassed Hell's dark border;
Vicious Scylla, Charybdis beneath the waters
  Did not cast down his noble soul.
It seemed harsh fate was vanquished by his patience
And he had drained the bitter-tasting bowl;
It seemed that Heaven had wearied of its vengeance
  And deep in slumber brought this man
Back to the wished-for cliffs from his wild ventures.
He woke—and did not know his fatherland.

(Essays, 233–34)

In fact, the city that Batyushkov returned to was hardly changed from the place he had known before the war. He took up residence with his beloved aunt Ekaterina Fyodorovna Muravyova in her house on the Fontanka River in the center of the city, and he spent much time with the Olenins on their estate at Priutino just outside the capital. But he didn't feel at home. Soon after arriving, he wrote to his older sister Anna:

> I don't know yet what my fate is to be; I haven't yet been transferred to the Guards, on which the possibility of my retirement depends. I won't weary you with complaints about my success in military service. Can you believe that I can serve as an example [of bad luck] in the army? But let's leave that, and put it right if we can. They are promising me a government place as a civilian: my old job in the library, which I will be glad to take, or anything else that turns up.
>
> (*SP, 376*)

But if fate was not looking after Batyushkov as he would have wished, he in turn found it hard to settle to anything. His old torment of depression dogged his steps. At about this time, he wrote a long verse tale (the longest of all his poems) called "The Traveler and the Stay-at-Home," a largely satirical story that expresses something of his own predicament. First conceived during his stay in London, it was completed after his return to Russia. The subject is not unlike that of La Fontaine's fable "The Two Pigeons," juxtaposing a footloose and foolish wanderer with a contented stay-at-home. It opens with a personal statement:

> I've seen the world, and now,
> A quiet stay-at-home, I sit and ponder
> By my own fireside how
> Hard it can be to keep your life in order;

How hard to spend your days on your own patch
When you have roamed about on land and water,
Seeing and knowing everything, then coming back
    No wiser and no better
    To your ancestral plot:
    A slave to empty fancies,
You live condemned to seek . . . but seek for what?
So let me tell the tale of one such traveler.

(Essays, 308)

The story, set in classical Greece, follows the fortunes of Filaletos, who leaves his brother Cliton at home on their modest estate on the outskirts of Athens. Spurred on by ambition and curiosity, he travels the ancient world, talks with religious leaders and philosophers, fails to find any real truth, returns to Greece, suffers all kinds of hardship, and eventually makes his way back to Athens. Here Batyushkov, who has been telling his story in a detached satirical voice, suddenly brings himself into the picture, likening this homecoming to his own return to St. Petersburg:

He was a Greek, of course, and loved his country;
He knelt and kissed the earth with joy and tears;
Beside himself with happiness, he accosted
    The houses and the trees! . . .
I too, my friends, I felt my heart rejoice
When tossed by fate's upheavals
From foreign shores, I reached my native place
And saw again the Admiralty Needle,
The house on the Fontanka . . . and the faces
Dearer to me than anything on earth! . . .
I too . . . But we must speak of Filaletos . . .

(Essays, 316)

And Filaletos has a rough time of it, even in Athens. He gets involved
in a violent debate about war and peace, setting the citizens against
him, and only just manages to escape into the welcoming arms of
his brother. Now at last all seems to be set for a properly moralized
ending, where the overambitious Filaletos will learn to appreciate
the superior wisdom of the stay-at-home Cliton. But no, for Baty-
ushkov, with his knowledge of *skuka* and his itchy feet, this happy
ending cannot work. Like the hero of the *Odyssey*, Filaletos is des-
tined to keep traveling:

> And just five days went by
> Before our Greek, tired of the same old meadow
> And the same faces every day—
> Can you believe it!—pined for his lost freedom.
> He started to explore the nearby woods
> And climbed the local mountains,
> All through the night and day wandered the roads
> Then secretly made his way to Athens
> To yawn
> Again in that sweet town
> And chat with Sophists about this and that;
> And then, on hearing from some scholars
> That in the world there is a land
> Where spring is never-ending,
> Went to find roses—among the Hyperboreans.
> Cliton and Cliton's wife from their front door
> Shouted in vain to stop him in his tracks:
> "Brother, dear brother, for God's sake, please come back!
> What do you hope to find so far from home?
> New miseries? What are you running from?
> Do you resent our friendship, cruel man?
> Stay here, dear brother, stay, dear Filaletos!"

No good.—The oddball simply shrugged his shoulders
And disappeared without a backward glance.

(*Essays, 319*)

Batyushkov, however, did not set off again immediately. Encouraged by the Olenin circle, he wrote the first two of a series of literary essays that would be published in the first (prose) volume of his works a couple of years later. The first of these takes the form of a letter to a cousin of Batyushkov's patron and mentor Mikhail Muravyov. Subsequently printed as the foreword to an edition of Muravyov's works, it presents and praises his various writings in a tone of gratitude and family piety, insisting on his public-spiritedness, his humane values, and his cult of feeling. It is a personal essay, in which Batyushkov clearly speaks in his own name.

The second and more interesting of these prose works is quite different. "A Walk to the Academy of Fine Art" is presented as a letter too, but it is supposedly written by a somewhat elderly Petersburger to a friend living in the country, and it presents a series of dialogues between the author and other visitors to the academy show, notably an enthusiastic young artist and an old reactionary who professes contempt for new Russian art. Discussing just a few of the works on display, the essay is much concerned with the relation between the new art of Russia and the models provided by antiquity and Western Europe. As such it clearly relates to Batyushkov's own poetic practice. Just as the poet had found a new voice for himself by imitating and translating Tibullus, Tasso, Parny, and others, so the artists find inspiration by imitating or copying the great works of other cultures; as one of the interlocutors puts it, "these artists are original in their imitation" (*Essays*, 57).

The text begins and ends with references to the great German art historian Johann Joachim Winckelmann; the dominant position adopted by Batyushkov is close to Winckelmann's neoclassicism.

But this does not imply that Russian culture is inevitably derivative and therefore inferior. On the contrary, the very city of St. Petersburg, superior in its unified grandeur to decrepit Paris and smoky London, is like a proclamation of the new mission of Russia. Here again we find a hymn of praise to Peter the Great, together with a reflection on the creation of the city that anticipates the opening of Pushkin's "Bronze Horseman": "Here will be a city—he said—the wonder of the world. I shall summon all the arts and crafts here. Here the arts and crafts, civic institutions and laws will vanquish nature herself. He spoke—and St. Petersburg rose from the wild marshland" (*Essays*, 73–74).[1] The essay breathes the patriotism of one who had marched into Paris with Alexander I. The equestrian statue of Peter (Pushkin's bronze horseman) may be the work of a Frenchman (Falconet), but as a visitor says, "it gallops like Russia!" (*Essays*, 81).

Meanwhile Batyushkov was continuing to write poems. A few of these continue in an earlier vein, imitating the French verse of Parny or Millevoye in very free translations. These are mostly love poems, often taking the Russian poet into the realms of imagination rather than reflecting his actual existence. "Bacchante," for instance, condenses a long text by Parny, "Les Déguisements de Vénus," roughly translating one of Parny's "tableaux," to create a Russian poem that enjoyed great success in its day. It is a throwback to his earlier Epicurean mode, though more frankly erotic than any earlier poems, but it comes oddly after the somber notes first sounded in the epistle to Dashkov about the burning of Moscow:

BACCHANTE

All to Erigone's feast
They run, the devotees of Bacchus;
Noisily the woods repeat

Moans of pleasure, shrieks and clapping.
In a dark wild forest glade,
Left behind, a young nymph lingers;
I give chase—she runs away,
An antelope, light and nimble.

Zephyrs tousle her young hair
Wound about with ivy tendrils;
Boldly the wind sweeps up her skirts,
Knotting them in a dense tangle.

Yellow hops go subtly winding
All around her lovely form,
And her cheeks are fairly glowing
With the crimson of the rose.

Grapes in purple juice all melting
Stain the mouth she opens wide—
Crazy, utterly enchanting,
Poison to the heart on fire.

I give chase—she runs away
An antelope, light and nimble,
I catch her, and she falls to earth!
Her head rests upon her timbrel!
And the devotees of Bacchus
Wildly shrieking, hurry by,
Through the forest raising echoes—
Cries of pleasure, *Evoe*.

(*Essays*, 288–89)

A very different note is struck by another imitation from the French written at about the same time. "The Last Spring" is loosely based on a poem by the contemporary French poet Charles-Hubert Millevoye, "La Chute des feuilles," but where Millevoye has a love-sick hero fading away in harmony with the dying year, Batyushkov, in a manner reminiscent of Petrarch, contrasts human suffering with the springtime renewal of nature:

THE LAST SPRING

Bright May is playing in the fields,
The stream begins to chatter freely,
And Philomela's brilliant voice
Has charmed the dark wood's melancholy:
Now everything drinks in new life!
You only, singer of love, are sad!
And deep in your sad heart you hide
The knowledge of your coming end;
With feeble steps you make your way
This one last time over the fields,
Taking your leave of them today
And of your wasted homeland's woods.
"Farewell! you groves and valleys dear,
Rivers and fields that I call home!
Spring has returned, and I can see
My fated hour of death has come.
This was the prophecy I heard
At Epidaurus: you will hear
For the last time the cooing birds,
The halcyon's quiet melody.
The twigs will once again be green,
The fields be garlanded with flowers,
And the first roses will be seen—
And you will share their dying hour.
The time is close . . . Sweet flowers in bloom,
Why do you haste to fade and die?
Cover the melancholy tomb

Where my decaying dust will lie.
Cover the road that leads us there,
So that no friendly eye can see.
But if a grieving Delia
Should come near to the place, then breathe
Your sweetness through the empty air
That lies all round and charm my sleep,
My sweet sleep, with your melody
Of languorously trembling leaves."
The flowers did not fade in the fields,
The halcyons with their quiet song
Mingled their voices with the leaves—
But the youth dwindled and was gone!
And friendship never shed a tear
Where his dear dust slept in the shade,
And Delia never came to see
The desolate tomb where he was laid;
Only the shepherd at high noon,
When he had set his flock to graze,
Troubled with his unhappy tune
The deathly silence of the grave.

(Essays, 234–35)

This poem, which left its mark on Pushkin (discussed later in this chapter), is more characteristic than "Bacchante" of the Batyushkov of 1815. Like "Bacchante," it is set in an antique world, with Delia, halcyons,[2] and a musical shepherd, but its melancholy tonality sets the tone for a number of directly personal love poems written later the same year, when Batyushkov was coming to terms with the sad end of his one serious involvement with a woman about which we know anything.

This was his love for Anna Fyodorovna Furman, whom he had met in the house of the Olenins, her protectors, in 1812. He had carried her image with him throughout his Napoleonic campaigns; on returning to St. Petersburg, he met her again, and his love flared up with new force. She was now twenty-two, a beauty without a fortune, and her friends and protectors would have been glad to see her married to Batyushkov. But he could see all too well that she did not feel for him as he did for her, and he did not want to insist, the more so since he was not in a position to offer her a financially stable future. He later explained his situation in a letter to his aunt, Ekaterina Muravyova, written in August 1815, by which time Anna had left St. Petersburg to join her father in Dorpat (now Tartu, in Estonia) and Batyushkov himself had been taken by military service to Kamenets-Podolsk in Bessarabia in the far south of Russia:

> The most important obstacle is that I cannot sacrifice what I hold most dear. I do not deserve her and cannot make her happy with my character and my lack of means. That is a truth that neither you, nor anything in the world can overcome, of course. All the circumstances are against me. I must submit without complaining to the holy will of God, which is sent to try me. I cannot stop loving her. Your last lines made me suffer. I do not like this journey of hers, dear aunt. I wish I could see or know that she was in St. Petersburg, with good people, and near to you. Forgive me this worrisome grief. You are the only woman on earth to whom I can be sincere, but even to you I am afraid to open my heart. I am indeed very sad. One can live without hope, but to see only tears all around one, to see the suffering of everything the heart holds dear, that is a torment that you too know: you have loved.
>
> (SP, 385)

It is in the light of this letter that one can read a group of poems written in Kamenets in the summer of 1815. The first of these was attached to the letter just quoted, no doubt to show his aunt what he felt about Anna, though the feeling is much less bitterly expressed here than in the letter. What Batyushkov calls "memory of the heart" is stronger now than loss and grief:

MY GUARDIAN SPIRIT

Memory of the heart! more potent
Than reason's mournful memory,
Often with your allure of sweetness
You carry me off to a far country.
And I remember words so tender,
Remember eyes as blue as the sky,
Remember too the golden tresses
Of hair that curls so carelessly;
Remember too the simple costume
Of my unparalleled shepherdess,
The tender vision, unforgotten,
That stays with me at every step.
Love gives to me this guardian spirit
To soften separation's blows
And, when I sleep, to haunt my pillow
And ease my sorrowful repose.

(Essays, 220–21)

A second poem also accompanied the letter to Muravyova. Here Batyushkov goes back over the years of his campaigns and travels, his return to Russia, and even his present situation in the south by the river Tiras (the Greek name for the Dniester, which flows by Kamenets). The juxtaposition of death and resurrection at the end of this poem of longing carries one back to an earlier and happier love poem, "Convalescence" (see chapter 2):

PARTING

In vain I left behind my father's country,
    My bosom friends, the glitter of art,
And in the soldier's tent, the noise of battle
Sought to find comfort for a suffering heart.
Ah! alien skies cannot make good love's wounds!
    In vain from land to land
I made my way, and heard the fearsome sound
    Of seas that crashed against the strand.
In vain, when fate had torn me from the shores
    Of my great northern city's river,
I came again to Moscow's ruined squares,
Moscow, where once I breathed the air of freedom!
    In vain I fled from northern deserts
And the weak comfort of a glacial sun
To where the Tiras glitters as it runs
    Between the hills enriched by Ceres
    In lands where ancient races feasted.
    In vain—one image haunts me still:
    The unforgettable dear girl
    Whose name will be forever sacred,
She whose blue eyes contain the universe,
Making a heaven on earth in their reflection,
Whose lovely voice, whose sweetly sounding words
    Are death to me, and resurrection.

(*Essays, 231–32*)

A much fuller picture of Batyushkov's recent years is given in a long poem entitled "Elegy." When it was first published in the poet's collected works in 1817, this piece bore the title "Memories: A Fragment," where the title word (*vospominaniia*) is the plural form of the title of the much earlier poem that I have translated as "Remembering" (discussed in chapter 2). In the 1817 edition, the two poems appear side by side. "Remembering" looked back to the campaign of 1807–1808 and Batyushkov's love for the merchant's daughter in Riga; "Memories" (or "Elegy") tells of his war service and travels through France, England, and Sweden in 1813–1814, relating all this to his love for Anna. However, to avoid embarrassment, he chose in 1817 to publish only the first part of the poem given below, where the unspecific reference to a "guardian angel" remains relatively discreet. In its full version, "Elegy" speaks more clearly of the poet's failure to win Anna's love. This unhappiness is related to his desertion by the Muses—ironically, in view of the fact that the loss of Anna seems to have sparked several of his most memorable poems. But "Elegy" begins with a clear and cheerless statement of the theme of lost inspiration, leading to a suggestion of the irreparable psychological damage done to the unloved poet:

ELEGY

I feel my gift for poetry is gone,
The muse has quenched the flame once lit in heaven;
    Life's sad experience has unveiled
A desert that my eyes had never seen,
My orphaned genius drives me out to fields
Where nothing grows, impenetrable shades,
Where I can find no sign of happiness,
Neither the secret joys, nor the dreams beyond meaning
    That Phoebus' favorites know from youth,
No friendship, love, no songs of the sweet muses
Which once assuaged my heart's deep grief
Like lotus blossom, with enchanting power.
    I do not recognize myself

Weighed down by this new sadness.
Like one cast on the rocks by the wild waves,
Who sees with horror the wreckage of his boat,
Interrogates the dark with trembling hands
And slips along the brink of the abyss,
The mad wind scattering his pleading speech,
　　　His groans and cries . . . just so I stand
On the edge of ruin and call out for help
To you, my last hope, you my consolation!
　　　Last friend of my poor heart!
　　　Among life's storms and tribulations
My guardian angel, given me by god! . . .
I hid your image in my soul, a token
Of the world's beauty, the creator's grace.
With your name on my lips I flew to arms
Seeking a wreath of glory or an end;
In times of terror, on the field of Mars,
I gave you the pure tribute of my heart;
　　　In peace and war, through the wide earth,
　　　Your loving image followed me,
Inseparable from a grieving wanderer.
How often in the stillness, full of you,
In woods where Juvisy stands proud above the river
And the Seine pours its silver crystal through the flowers,
How often, amid the noisy, carefree crowd
In the capital of luxury, among the stars,
I quite forgot the magic sirens' song
And with a longing heart dreamed just of you.
　　　I uttered your beloved name
　　　In Albion's cool groves,
　　　And taught the echo to repeat it
　　　On Richmond's flowering fields.

Places whose very wildness is your charm,
O stones of Sweden, Scandinavian deserts,
The ancient home of courage and of virtue!
You heard my vows, the accents of my love
And often fed a wanderer's meditations
When the pink radiance of the dawning day
Reflected in Trolletana's lonely waters
  The distant cliffs of granite shores,
The huts of shepherds and of fishermen
  Through the thin mist of morning.

(Essays, 212–13)

The poem breaks off here with a line of suspension points in the first published version. The original version goes on to a much clearer statement of the poet's unhappy love since his return to St. Petersburg:

How joyfully I came back to my homeland
With you alone filling my heart and mind!
"Here I shall find peace for my soul," I said,
"An end to troubles and the wandering life."
O how my lying dreams led me astray!
  For happiness once more betrayed me
In love and friendship and in everything
  That made life sweet for me,
  All that I'd longed for secretly!
There is an end to wandering, not to sorrows!
My heart discovered in your longed-for presence
  New sufferings and torments
  Worse than the pangs of parting,
And worse than everything. I could detect
In broken conversations, in your silences,

> In your unhappy gaze,
> And in the secret pain of downcast eyes,
>   Your smile and even your cheerful words,
>   Signs of a heart oppressed by sorrow . . .
>
> No! no! Life is a burden without hope.
> If only I could lavish on your soul
> The lasting flowers of love and friendship,
> Sacrifice everything to you, take pride in you
> And in your happiness and loving eyes,
>   Find gratitude and happiness
> In every word or smile or look of yours
> And at your feet forget like a bad dream
> The world, fame, bygone cares and grief!
> What is my life without you, without hope,
> Friendship or love, the objects of my worship? . . .
>   And lacking them, the muse
>   Has quenched the flame of inspiration.

(Essays, 536–37)

Reading these desolate lines, it is hard not to see in them an anticipation of the much more total collapse that was to strike down Batyushkov some seven years later.

In another poem written at much the same time, the sad memories of the past give way to a golden dream of a no doubt impossible future. The poem's title, "Tauris," was the poetic Russian name for the Crimea. This area had been annexed by Russia some thirty years earlier, and was to become a popular resort, Russia's equivalent of the Mediterranean, far removed from the "immense Palmyra" of St. Petersburg. Batyushkov's poem is one of the first of a long line of Russian evocations of this golden land; it was a favorite poem of Pushkin's (who was soon to be exiled in Southern Russia and would visit the Crimea). According to Pushkin, the lines about Aquarius were particularly dear to Batyushkov himself. It is generally supposed that the poem is addressed to Anna Furman, though it contains nothing relating specifically to her; it could equally be a poem to an imagined woman:

TAURIS

Dear friend, dear angel! let us take refuge there,
Where quiet waters lap the shores of Tauris,
And Phoebus lights for them the holy places
Of ancient Hellas with his loving rays.
    There we, by fate rejected,
Equal in both unhappiness and love,
Beneath the sweet skies of that southern land
Shall feel no more the blows of cruel fortune.
And think no more of honors or of wealth.
Under cool maples rustling in the meadows,
Where squadrons of wild horses gallop freely
Seeking cool waters bubbling though the earth,
Where the wayfarer gladly shuns the heat
To the murmur of branches, desert birds and waters,
There we shall find ourselves a simple cabin,
A homely spring, flowers, a rustic plot.
O you, last presents of indulgent fortune,
Our blazing hearts greet you a hundredfold!
Fitter for love than the palaces of marble
In the immense Palmyra of the north!
And whether spring goes shining through the fields,
Or torrid summer scorches up the harvest,
Or old Aquarius, tipping his frigid urn,
    Pours rustling rain, gray fog and darkness,

O joy! you are with me to greet the sunlight,
Leaving behind our sweet bed with the day,
    Glowing and fresh, like a wild rose,
With me you share the work, the care, the feasting.
With me at dusk, beneath the quiet dark,
With me, always with me—your charming eyes
I see, I hear your voice, in your hand resting,
    My hand can lie all day, all night.
I catch with longing the voluptuous breathing
    Of your red lips. and if a little
Your hair is ruffled by a fleeting Zephyr,
Unveiling to my gaze a snowy breast,
    Your friend hardly dares breathe, he stands
And looks down to the ground, amazed and silent.

(Essays, 232–33)

Batyushkov did not in fact visit the Crimea until 1822, by which time he was seriously ill. In 1815, there was no possibility of a happy escape with Anna to a southern paradise. Meanwhile, the clash between hope of renewal and acceptance of reality is the subject of one more memorable short poem of the same summer. When first published, it had an epigraph from Petrarch, and the Russian poem in fact resembles Petrarch's sonnet "Not the stars that wander the calm sky" ("Nè per sereno ciel ir vaghe stelle"), where none of the beauties of the world can comfort the lovesick poet:

WAKING
—————

Zephyr scatters the last shreds of sleep
From eyes sealed fast by dreams.
But I am not wakened to happiness

By Zephyr's quiet wings.
Neither the rosy light's sweet rays,
Apollo's morning heralds,
Nor the soft blue of heaven's face,
Nor scents borne from the fields,
Nor the swift flight of my brave horse
On the sloping velvet lawns,
The hounds' call and the song of horns
Around the desolate shore—
Nothing can bring cheer to my soul,
My soul alarmed by dreams;
Proud reason cannot still the voice
Of love with its cold speech.

(Essays, 230–31)

Batyushkov had been on leave from the army since his return from Paris, first in St. Petersburg, then in Khantonovo, where he set in train the rebuilding of the house—with some help from Napoleonic prisoners of war. But eventually, in June 1815, he had to return to the service in Kamenets-Podolsk as adjutant to General Bakhmetev, with whom he had embarked on the campaign of 1813–1814. He was not too cheerful about his prospects, writing to Gnedich:

The posting to Kamenets is not particularly flattering. I have no right to happiness of course, but it is painful to spend the best days of my life on the road, with no benefit to myself or to others; better to be fighting, it seems to me. And the most painful thing (and don't go thinking these are just empty words) is to be cut off from literature, from the life of the mind, from the pleasant habits of life, and from friends.

(SPP, 292)

The Return of Odysseus   \ 145

And indeed this period of nonactive military service did prove wearisome. At times, it is true, Batyushkov paints a romantic picture of his new surroundings. In a short text with a long title, "Memory of Places, Battles and Travels," he describes the view from the headquarters where he is stationed:

> The views of the ruins of the old fortress and of the new fortifications are beautiful. There are lofty towers with sharp pinnacles, half in ruins, covered with moss and with the wormwood which grows very tall in these southern latitudes; fortifications and bastions surrounded, or rather encircled, by a fast-flowing river which occasionally tumbles over waterfalls—the noise and sparkling streams soften the military gloom and monotony of the fortress buildings. In one place there is a mill, in another a ford where a great herd is crossing, and a little further off a spring cascading from the rocks; all around there is a multitude of children and women carrying yokes with buckets and crowds of Jews leaning on white sticks in the most picturesque attitude.
>
> (SP, 179)

All well and good, but alas! The human element in this landscape had little to offer. In the same letter to his aunt in which he writes about his feelings for Anna Furman, Batyushkov gives a rather cheerless, though humorous, picture of his life in the distant provinces:

> I have been here six weeks, and I haven't spoken to a single woman. You can see what Kamenets society is like. Apart from the officials and their wives and children, the civil servants and the cooks, two or three colonels, silent officers and a whole crowd of Jews, there is no one. There is a theatre; imagine what it is like: when it rains the

spectators take out their umbrellas, the wind whistles in all directions and with splendid drunken actors and a fiddle the orchestra produces a very special kind of harmony . . . All my joys and pleasures are in memory. The present is tedious, the future is known only to God, but the past is ours.

(SP, 386–87)

But this tedium, as one can perhaps guess from the humor of these lines, was a stimulus to writing. In a rather gloomy letter written from Kamenets in December to Zhukovsky, Batyushkov, complaining of his chaotic nomadic life, remarks: "I am ready to part company with the muses altogether, if I didn't find in them some consolation for my unhappiness" (*SP*, 388. "Unhappiness" is in Russian the untranslatable *toska*, a combination of grief and longing.). As we have seen, it was in Kamenets that he composed his most important sequence of love poems. The epistle "To My Friends" (cited in the introduction), written shortly before the Kamenets episode, suggests that he was already gathering his poems together with a view to publication. But these southern months also produced some important prose writings, which would occupy much of the first volume of his *Essays in Prose and in Verse*, published two years later.

As ever, Batyushkov was self-deprecating about these essays, writing to Zhukovsky: "All of this was scribbled here out of boredom, with no books or other materials" (*SP*, 390). They include reminiscences, connected above all with Ivan Petin, for whom he had written the elegy "Shade of a Friend." In the "Memories of Petin," already quoted several times in the preceding chapters, he recalls with great feeling the times he spent with his friend in the army and in Moscow, trying to sum up the life of a man whose character and fate he admired and envied. Was it not better, he asks, that

Petin should die in action while still young? His questions reflect back on his own situation:

> What do we lose, dying in the prime of life on the field of honor and glory, in the sight of thousands of people who have faced danger with us? A few brief moments of pleasure, perhaps, but also the agonies of ambition, and the experience of life which awaits us like a fearsome specter in our middle years.
>
> (*Essays, 398–99*)

Most of the essays, however, are on literary subjects or more general philosophical questions. There are essays on the great Italians, Petrarch, Tasso, and Ariosto, and one on Batyushkov's Russian hero, the poet and polymath Mikhailo Lomonosov, whose pioneering achievements he set alongside those of Peter the Great. The essay on Lomonosov stresses his passion for learning, his burning desire for literary fame, but also his relatively humble beginnings in the far north of Russia. These two strands—belief in poetry and the influence of the poet's early years—are taken up at greater length in an essay entitled "Some Thoughts on the Poet and Poetry." Here Batyushkov writes of the importance of first impressions, including those of climate, and of the ideal poetic way of life (the quiet of the countryside rather than the bustle of cities). The true poet is seen as a rare genius in his sensibility and his ability to communicate his feelings to others. Communication is indeed the essence of poetry:

> In the moment of inspiration, in the sweet moment of poetic enchantment, I would never have picked up a pen if I had found a heart capable of feeling what I feel; if I could communicate to it all my secret reflections and the full freshness of my dreams, and make it vibrate with the same strings that have sounded in my own heart. Where can one find a heart able to share with us all our feelings

and sensations? We cannot find it, and we have recourse to the art of expressing our thoughts, in the sweet hope that somewhere on earth there are kind hearts and cultivated minds for which a powerful and noble feeling, an apt expression, a beautiful verse and a page of living, eloquent prose are the true treasures of life.

(*Essays, 20–21*)

Batyushkov's ideal is still Montaigne, whose essays are a continuing conversation with posterity. One is reminded of his younger contemporary, Evgeny Baratynsky, who wrote in one of his poems:

> . . . one day
> A distant fellow-man will read my words
> And find my being, and, who knows, my soul
> Will raise an echo in his soul, and I,
> Who found a friend in my own time,
> Will find a reader in posterity. [3]

Friendship was the great value for Batyushkov, as for many of his fellow poets. And if poetry was to be a conversation with friends, real or to come, then the great rule was to be genuine: "Write as you live, and live as you write." This is the burden of "To My Friends," where Batyushkov writes:

> But friends will find my feelings here,
> The story of my passions,
> Delusions of my mind and heart;
> Cares, worries, sorrows of my earlier years,
> And light-winged pleasures.

His ambition, no doubt an impossible one, was to have his friends say of him: "He lived just as he wrote" (*Essays*, 200).

How to live is the topic of Batyushkov's most important essay of 1815, "Some Thoughts on Morality, Founded on Philosophy and Religion." The significance he attached to this slightly longer piece is indicated by the fact that he gave it the final position in the volume of his prose writings. It represents a major change in his view of life. In earlier poems and letters, he had written of his "little philosophy" for living, an Epicurean enjoyment of the moment, without too much concern for larger questions. Even there, however, this carpe diem philosophy was in fact accompanied by a degree of anxiety about personal and public destinies. "Some Thoughts on Morality" offers a more tragic vision of things, and gives a hint of his later despair and mental collapse. It reflects in particular the pain Batyushkov had felt on witnessing the French invasion of Russia and the burning of Moscow (already the subject in 1813 of his great epistle to Dashkov).

The essay speaks of a conversion from the frivolity of carefree youth to the serious concerns of maturity. What Batyushkov calls the "age of reading" (i.e., enthusiastic openness to the various visions of the world) gives way to the "age of doubts," where the individual realizes the need for solid values that will stand the test of reality. This is particularly urgent because he and his contemporaries live "unfortunately . . . in an unhappy age when human wisdom is not sufficient to cope with the ordinary concerns of the most simple citizen." We have seen, he says, "the terrible ruins of the capital, amidst the even more terrible ruins of all order and the sufferings of all humanity throughout the enlightened world" (*Essays*, 184). This destruction is all the more fearful because it has been inflicted on Europe by a nation that was taken as a model of civilization and enlightenment.

To ease his doubt, then, Batyushkov reviews the currently fashionable philosophies, the writings of the ancient Stoics and

Epicureans, of course, but also a series of modern French thinkers: Duclos, La Rochefoucauld, Helvétius, and the whole materialistic school, whose morality is founded on interest and pleasure. None of these can satisfy the seeker of lasting values. Even the Epicureanism of the great Montaigne is found wanting: Batyushkov aligns himself rather with the Christian apologist Pascal's double refutation of the Epicurean Montaigne and the Stoic Epictetus. Among recent writers, Jean-Jacques Rousseau, although "gifted with great genius," provides an eloquent example of the failure of philosophy to deal with human weakness; his posthumous (and for Batyushkov shocking) *Confessions* demonstrate the inadequacy of the simple love of virtue: "So a man born for virtue committed a terrible, previously unheard-of, crime, a crime engendered by human wisdom." There is only one true remedy for human weakness, and that is faith: "Only religion could comfort and calm the suffering man; he knew and felt this truth, but led astray by his own pride, he constantly turned away from this light yoke of salvation" (*Essays*, 191–92). And Batyushkov is happy to see in his native Russia the power of a Christian country to overcome the rationalist infidels:

> The spear and the saber, bloodied by holy water on the banks of the quiet Don, have flashed in the house of dishonor, in sight of the temples of *reason, fraternity and liberty*, erected by atheism; and the banner of Moscow, of faith and of honor, stands in the place of the greatest crime against God and humanity.
>
> (*Essays, 195–96*)

Looking back on the war, Batyushkov seems now to be leaning toward a traditional, not to say reactionary, view of society and history, a view that was at odds with those of many of his liberal or radical friends. Certainly, as he himself admitted to Zhukovsky, he was not the person he had been: "My character has changed greatly: I have become thoughtful, silent, quiet to the point of stupidity, and even uncaring" (*SP*, 391). Put more positively, his experience had brought him a new seriousness, which expressed itself in his advice in the same letter to Zhukovsky not to content himself with ballads, but to seek out a form of poetry more worthy of his gifts. Younger poets, notably Pushkin and Vyazemsky, were dismayed to see Batyushkov abandoning the Epicurean stance of his earlier poetry. In a verse epistle, the fifteen-year-old Pushkin asked: "Why on his gold-stringed harp has the singer of joy fallen silent?" As he saw it, his elder's particular gift was for beautiful play rather than solemn public verse.[4] And the irreverent Vyazemsky lamented the change that had come over his once playful friend in a rather brutal letter:

> Zhukovsky scared me; now I can see that he was merely unwell, whereas you are sick. Perhaps Zhukovsky's unhappiness was the mother of his genius; yours—forgive me—is the mother of stupidity. Imagine a madman who picks a rose, taking away all its freshness and its scent—and then admires the stem. You are just like that madman; you are attempting to ruin the charm of your life . . . Be the Batyushkov you were, when I gave you a piece of my heart, or else don't expect me to love you, since I was born to love Batyushkov and not some other person.
>
> (*WP, 204*)

It may have been in response to reproaches of this kind that Batyushkov in this same crucial year of 1815 wrote a serious long epistle to Vyazemsky. Referring directly to the early death of the prince's friend Varvara Kokoshkina ("Lila," the subject of an elegy cited in chapter 3), and to the tragic events of 1812, in which his Moscow house ("the house of joy") had burned down, Batyushkov takes up the themes of his essay on morality: the inadequacy of worldly philosophy and the hope offered by faith ("Hope" is also the title of a short poem of 1815 on the same subject):

TO A FRIEND

Tell me, young thinker, what in this world will last?
    Where can good fortune live forever?
We have played among the phantoms of the dust
    And we have drained the cup of pleasure;

But where are they, those feasts, those golden times?
    Where are they now, the brimming glasses?
Where the bright wisdom of those worldly minds?
    Where your Falernian wine, our roses?

Where is your house, the house of joy? All gone.
    The place it stood is deep in nettles,
But I still know it, and my heart pours out
    Tribute to what it still remembers.

Where the city's constant noise is stilled
    And Venus' bright rays flood the darkness
Of northern skies, your melancholy friend
    Stands in the quiet night and wonders.

From my young days I served at the sweet shrine
    Of the divinities of pleasure,
But now I seek relief from passion's fire
    For my full heart in contemplation.

Can you believe it? Here, in the temple's ash,
    I lay aside the crown of revels

And often, stirred by feeling, all abashed,
    Hiding my face, I cry to heaven:

"On our brief road our path is lined with tombs,
    And every day is marked by losses.
On wings of joy we fly to seek our friends
    And find . . . just urns and funeral crosses."

Say, was it long ago that Lila here
    Dazzled your friends with her great beauty?
It seemed that kindly heaven had given to her
    All blessings granted to a mortal:

A calm, angelic nature, golden speech,
    Fine taste, the cheeks and eyes of Venus,
The open brow of a majestic muse,
    The charms of the unsullied graces.

And you, who shunned society's empty buzz,
    Delighted in her conversation
And plunged in quiet joy, admired this rose
    That flowered in the dusty desert.

Alas! the rose has faded like a dream;
    Suffering, she fell asleep forever;
In that dread hour she left the world behind,
    Fixing her eyes on her friend's features.

Perhaps friendship forgot that she had lived,
    And laughter dried the tears of sorrow,
Or the breath of slander in this sorry life
    Ruffled the purest shadow's surface.

So in this vain world all is vanity—
    Friendship, affection, all is fleeting.
But where, my friend is there a constant light?
    What is there that is pure, unfading?

In vain I asked the wisdom of the past
    And the obscure archives of Clio;
In vain I asked the sages of the earth—
    All answered me with vacant silence.

Like a feather on the wind swirled here and there,
    Or like a dust cloud on an eddy,
Or like a ship adrift among the waves
    And seeking vainly for the jetty,

Even so my mind drowned in a sea of doubt,
    All life's enjoyments had been banished,
My guardian spirit had gone, my lamp was out,
    And the bright muses all had vanished.

Fearful, I listened to the inner voice—
    And darkness fled, my eyes were opened,
And faith poured out her all-redeeming oil
    To light my lamp, all pure, all hopeful.

My way to the grave is lit as by the sun;
    On a firm footing I step forward,
And shaking dust and darkness from my gown,
    Soar to a better world in spirit.

(Essays, 250–53)

The moralizing here is emphatic enough, but it would be a mistake to imagine that the old irreverent Batyushkov had vanished forever. At the end of 1815 he was able to leave his dreary southern exile and return to Moscow, Khantonovo, and St. Petersburg, where in the next two years he would play a central role in the distinctly light-hearted operations of the new literary group, Arzamas.

06

ARZAMAS AND THE *ESSAYS*

Arzamas was a writers' circle that made its appearance in St. Petersburg in the autumn of 1815. The immediate stimulus for its creation was a play by A. A. Shakhovskoy, an active member of the Circle of Lovers of the Russian Word that Batyushkov had mocked in a number of writings, notably the "Vision on the Banks of Lethe." The play satirized Zhukovsky, and through him the innovative writers who followed in the footsteps of Karamzin. The Karamzinians fought back, and this time they went further and set up a society named mockingly after a provincial town in the Nizhny Novgorod district. The activities of the society were both a somewhat frivolous game and a serious literary enterprise. The members parodied the rituals of the Circle in their meetings, wearing red bonnets and composing comic obituaries for their opponents. They had a definite aim, which was "to bury the late Academy and the Circle of Destroyers of the Russian Word" (to quote the schoolboy Pushkin, soon to become a member). But also, as one of their number, S. S. Uvarov, remembered, "the purpose of this society, or rather of these conversations among friends, was essentially critical. The members devoted themselves to a strict analysis of literary works, applying to the national language and literature all the sources of ancient and foreign literature, seeking for the founding principles of a solid and independent theory of language, etc." (*WP*, 230). Among the two dozen members were some of the most important Russian writers of the period, including Zhukov-sky, Vyazemsky, the society poet Vasily Pushkin, his young nephew Aleksandr, and of course Batyushkov.

The members all adopted nicknames. The young Pushkin was "Cricket"; Batyushkov was "Achilles." This may have been a jokingly ironic reference to his small stature, but it also indicates that he was a champion of Arzamas. Living far from St. Peters-burg, for two years he was a corresponding member, whether in Kamenets, Moscow, or Khantonovo; in December 1815, he wrote to Zhukovsky that he was proud of his new name, but that for the time being Achilles would remain inactive "behind the crimson and black ships" (*SP*, 389). Even from a distance, however, he par-ticipated in the society's activities, submitting in 1816 his newly composed dialogue, "An Evening at Kantemir's" for his colleagues to discuss. And in March 1817 he sent Vyazemsky a "Question for Arzamas," a playful epigram juxtaposing three different poets called Pushkin (*not* including the subsequently famous Aleksandr). Later on, once he had returned to St. Petersburg in the late summer of 1817, he was an active member, since this new grouping corre-sponded very well with his own literary orientation.

Meanwhile, at the end of 1815, Batyushkov was able at last to shake the dust of Kamenets from his feet. He obtained leave from General Bakhmetev, and made his way to Moscow, where he was lodged by his hospitable relation Ivan Muravyov-Apostol, and greeted by Vyazemsky and other old friends. Soon he found that he had been transferred, as he had long wished, to the Guards, but this appointment did not last long, since in April 1816 he was allowed to take the retirement from military service that he had requested. He was now a collegiate assessor (the equivalent of major in the army), but this did not give him a position or a salary. For the next two years he mentions in letters his desire for some sort of government service that would give him security and allow him to feel that he was doing something useful and honorable. He was often ill, and constantly short of money, too poor to live permanently in either of the capitals. As a result, he would spend much of 1817 on his estate at Khantonovo in order to live more cheaply. And in the country, although oppressed by *skuka* and cold, he had more time to read and to write poetry.

In spite of illness and shortage of cash, these two years spent largely in Moscow and Khantonovo saw Batyushkov reach the peak of his literary career. In February 1816, he was elected with Zhukovsky to the Society of the Lovers of Literature, which had rejected him five years earlier. He marked the occasion with a speech, which was read at a meeting of the society, on the subject of "the influence of light verse on the language." This was partly a formal affair, with some rather blatant flattery of the members; Batyushkov wrote in a letter to Gnedich, parodying a line of Derzhavin: "I spoke the truth to donkeys with a smile" (*SP*, 400). But this "truth" was an important one for him, and he chose to place the speech at the head of the two-volume edition of his works that appeared the following year. The "light verse" of the title is the society verse that Batyushkov and his friends had written in imitation of Parny and other French poets. This is placed in opposition to the grander forms of poetry; where the epic or the ode demand a more formal, archaic style, epistles, elegies, and epigrams offer a more direct reflection of the language of modern polite society.

Citing a whole range of models, ancient and modern, from Catullus, Tibullus, and Propertius to Petrarch, Marot, Waller, and Derzhavin, Batyushkov remarks:

> In the lighter kind of poetry, the reader demands all possible perfection, purity of expression, elegance of style, supple and flowing verse; he demands truth of feeling and the strictest propriety in

every respect. . . . Beauty of style is essential here and nothing can take its place. It is a secret known only to talent and especially to the constant application of attention to one subject, since poetry of the lighter kind is a difficult art that demands a person's whole life and mental exertions.

(*Essays, 11–12*)

He goes on to note that this urbanity was cultivated in the great age of Catherine, "so auspicious to science and literature," and that those who practice it have profited from "the attentive reading of foreign authors, some of them ancient, others very recent." One can see how close this ideal was to Batyushkov's own practice.

An important element in the speech is patriotic pride in Russia, a pride heightened by the Napoleonic wars. The Society's essential aim, says Batyushkov, is to enrich "a language, so closely bound up with the civic education, the enlightenment and thence the prosperity of the most glorious and most extensive country in the world," and it pursues this aim "in the most ancient shrine of the national Muses, which is rising again from the ashes together with the capital of Russia and will eventually become worthy of its former greatness" (*SP*, 8). The cultivation of light verse therefore has its part to play in the creation of a sophisticated literary culture that will establish Russia alongside the prestigious cultures of Western Europe. The same ambition is expressed, as we saw earlier, in the dialogue "An Evening at Kantemir's," also written in 1816. This is a conversation between Antiokh Kantemir, a polyglot poet and Russian ambassador in Paris, and two French men of letters, Montesquieu and a character labeled "Abbé B." The Frenchmen express surprise that Kantemir writes poems in Russian, for them a barbarous tongue. The response is a hymn of praise to Peter the Great and to his literary equivalent Lomonosov. Writing some eighty years after Kantemir, Batyushkov can put into his mouth hopes and prophecies that are already being fulfilled—he even mischievously has the Abbé remark that to imagine the flourishing of civilization in Russia is comparable to imagining Russian troops marching into Paris (*SP*, 47). Russia's time, it is implied, has come.

Among other things, Kantemir remarks on the beauties of Russian popular culture: "We Russians have folk songs: they are filled with the tenderness and eloquence of the heart; you can see in them the quiet deep thoughtfulness that imparts an inexplicable charm to even the most unpolished productions of the northern muse" (*SP*, 46). In this period, Batyushkov, like many of his fellow poets, was showing a new interest in the themes and forms of Russian folk literature. In 1817 he asked Gnedich to send him some examples of traditional Russian poetry, since he was planning a poem called "The Water Sprite" or "Mermaid" ("Rusalka") set in the legendary days of Russian antiquity. A letter to Vyazemsky outlines the plot of this poem (*SP*, 413–14), but unfortunately the plan remained unrealized, and it was left to the young Pushkin to illustrate the genre a couple of years later with his pathbreaking *Ruslan and Lyudmila*. All that Batyushkov managed was a brief unfinished poem in which we see and hear a Russian soldier back from the wars in a part of Russia remote from his own native region—which he calls the "motherland." His nostalgic lament recalls that of the earlier poem, "The Prisoner." Here are the central stanzas of this fragmentary song (the original sounds more peasant-like than the translation):

> Sails on the water, where do you ply?—
> > To the holy motherland.
> Birds of the air, why does your band
> Soar up so high into the sky?—
> > To the woods of home we fly.

> All things living fly to their home,
>> But I must wander here,
>> I sing a sad song through my tears,
>> Along the roads and paths I roam
>> And sing a song of home.

(CP, 204)

In a similar vein, Batyushkov did homage to the "northern muse" with his free translation of the currently popular ancient poem previously translated into English by William Mason as the "Song of Harald the Valiant." This piece, taken from one of the sagas, is spoken by the eleventh-century Norwegian King Harald Sigurdson, known to the English as Harald Hardraade, who fell at the battle of Stamford Bridge in 1066. It tells of a heroic adventurer who is disdained (in the last line of every stanza) by a Russian maiden (see *Essays*, 287–88). The poem echoes the "nordic" sentiments expressed in "'On the Ruins of a Castle in Sweden" and in the central section of his very early poem "Dreaming," which Batyushkov kept reworking and expanding, evoking the romantic appeal of the old North, and confusing as he did so the very different worlds of Ossian and the sagas.

A good deal of his poetic output at this time, however, belonged more to the category he had labeled "light verse" in his speech of 1816. This includes a number of satirical epigrams, such as this one of 1815, directed against an unknown target:

> Pamphilus is merry at table,
> Though often at reason's expense:
> He owes his gay moods to his belly,
> To memory his flashes of sense.

(Essays, 305)

Or else there were little poems of friendship, including a quatrain that was sent with a bunch of flowers to "our Horace," the garden-loving poet Ivan Dmitriev:

Blizzards and frosts have come and gone—
Your trees and flowers are never blighted.
I know from Apollo and Aphrodite
In Horace's garden the roses live on.

(*Essays, 306*)

Both of these little pieces were included by Batyushkov—though with some hesitation—in the edition of his works that came out in 1817. The same is true of the "Epistle to Turgenev," a longer piece included in a letter of October 1816 to his close friend, the influential statesman Aleksandr Turgenev.[1] The poem is part of his successful attempt to persuade Turgenev to assist the widow of a war veteran and her daughter; after an appeal to his friend's generosity, Batyushkov goes on to present his two heroines in a familiarly free and varied style that seems to owe something to the masters of French light verse, not least La Fontaine:

. . . But who are *they*? Like it or not,
I'll tell you their whole gloomy story.
They are a widow and her daughter
        A pair that fate forgot;
There was a husband called Popov,
        The tsar's devoted soldier,
A poor man. Then he died. Free of
All debts, of course, he met his maker.
But in this world he left a wife
        With a young child, and only

His knapsack as a legacy . . .
    But here the poor aren't lonely!
Good folk came to their aid and fed
    The two of them, and warmed them,
And in a word, did what they could
    To shelter the poor orphans.
That's splendid! Marvelous!—Well, yes,
    But our sad world is hardly
A paradise, as grandpa says . . .
    In marched a foreign army,
And Moscow burned down to the ground,
And our poor widow woman, ruined,
Set off again with staff in hand . . .
And all the time her daughter grew,
And as she grew, her needs grew too;
Day followed day, they all just vanished,
The weeks and months, and they were famished.
The aged dame is sinking, while
Her daughter blossoms like a flower,
Like Grace itself, with lovely eyes
    And looks that overpower.
With Flora's roses in her cheeks,
And hair as fine as golden flax
Falling on alabaster shoulders.
Her every word is full of grace,
She lends a beauty to her dress,
But all her wealth is in her face,
    Her beauty is her dowry.
Never a crumb of bread or cake . . .
Turgenev, friend, for heaven's sake,
Help me to rescue loveliness,
Poverty and unhappiness!

They'll light a pure wax candle there
Before the holy face, of course.
Who will they pray for? I won't say,
        But you, my friend, can guess.

(Essays, 272–73)

In such epistles, poetic talk seems like a natural continuation of conversation; storytelling, humor, sentimental eloquence, commonsense remarks, and some semi-parodic description of female beauty mingle to create an entertaining discourse. In its ability to deal with such mundane subjects as poor relief, this light verse, as Batyushkov suggests, contributes to polishing the language of ordinary Russian speech. The same is true of a series of rather more jokey epistles of 1817 to an older member of Arzamas, Vassily Pushkin. Remembered now almost entirely as the uncle of his famous nephew, Vassily was in his day a leading society poet. The first piece is a quite trivial evocation of the old familiar boredom felt by Batyushkov in his country retreat:

I honestly don't know the date;
Time stands still, in bands of steel;
Boredom is happy to repeat:
        "It's time to drink your tea,
        Time for a meal, a sleep,
        Time to get out the sleigh."
"It's time for you to give up poetry"—
Reason keeps on at me day after day.

(CP, 250)

Another little poem from a letter written at much the same time praises Pushkin for his devotion to the light poetry—wine, women, and song—that Batyushkov had praised in his speech, and in which he had first found fame himself. Pushkin is compared here to the old models of French elegance, from the Renaissance poet Clément Marot to the chevalier de Boufflers, who had died only four years earlier, and with whom Batyushkov had himself been compared. The tone is humorous, but the sentiment seems to be sincere; the escape from "dark oblivion's greedy jaws" is a recurrent theme in Batyushkov's work:

Eternal youth is his whose voice
>   Sings Eros, love and wine,
>   Who plucks sweet pleasure's fleeting rose
In the gay gardens of Boufflers, Marot.
He may be harassed by vile coughs and gout
>   And the creditors' unholy throng,
>   And toil away all the day long
>   To keep the booksellers supplied.
>   Once dead, forgotten!—Not a bit—
>   Posterity will grasp the truth:
On what, and how and where the poet lived,
Where he expired, where his poor dust is laid.
>   Believe me, fate will rescue him
>   From dark oblivion's greedy jaws
>   And bear to immortality
>   The man, his life, his works.

(CP, 212–13)

A third squib, which bears the grand title "Epistle from a Practical Sage to the Sage of Astafievo and the Pushkinistic Sage," was written later in the same year, still from Khantonovo. Included in a letter to Vyazemsky (the "sage of Astafievo"), it is addressed jointly to him and Vassily Pushkin and promises to visit Astafievo, in spite of bad weather. Batyushkov writes in prose: "Some feeble souls like yours complain about the weather; the true sage declares . . ." after which comes the verse passage:

> Happy whose paradise within
> Is not disturbed by passion's showers
> Bright May will always shine on him
> And Life will never grudge him flowers!
> Remember how Epictetus in a ragged cloak
> Didn't know that the barometer foretold foul weather
> Or that the universe's values shook
> And Rome was poised to swallow the world's freedom.
> His flesh and spirit tough from constant labor,
> Heat did not make him sweat or rainstorms soak him.
> I shall be tougher far than Epictetus.
> Wrapped in a cloak of patience,
> I shall appear before you
> With the first light of day.
> Yes! yes! you'll see me standing on your threshold
> Wearing a stoical expression.
> I won't be short of things to say!
> Ideas from Seneca,
> The gift of eloquence from Sokovnín,
> The social graces from Ilyín,[2]
> And my philosophy . . . from the pharmacy.

(CP, 250–51)

These are all poems of friendship—a supreme value for Batyush-kov. In March 1817, he wrote to Gnedich that when he had finished his current poem ("Tasso Dying") he would write no more—"except letters to friends: that is my real genre, as I have finally realized" (*SP*, 403). And indeed these letters (more than three hundred have survived) are among his best writing, by turns graphically descriptive, self-mockingly witty, and sincerely felt. It is interesting in particular to look at the letters to his close literary friends—Gnedich, Vyazemsky, and Zhukovsky; all are familiar and full of life, but the tone changes with the recipient, more ebullient and youthfully malicious with his oldest friend Gnedich, affectionately serious with the somewhat older and more prestigious Zhukovsky.

Much of the correspondence with Gnedich at this time was taken up with a major event in Batyushkov's life, the publication of his works. The idea seems to have come spontaneously and unexpectedly from Gnedich in the summer of 1816. He offered not only to edit the volumes, but to print them at his own expense, paying the author an advance. His friend at first treated this as a joke, saying that Gnedich would ruin himself, but in the end the offer was too tempting to refuse, and it was agreed to publish two volumes, respectively, of prose and verse. The prose was ready for publication by the beginning of 1817, but both volumes were published several months later. In the end, Gnedich made a reasonable profit on the undertaking, but the impoverished Batyushkov received only a modest sum.

Gnedich proved to be a conscientious and a highly sympathetic editor. Based in St. Petersburg, he took on all the necessary tasks of publication, consulting his country friend about the choice and the ordering of texts, suggesting corrections, organizing a subscription (rather against Batyushkov's wishes), and of course writing a preface. He at first proposed an enthusiastic presentation, possibly on the lines of the following draft for a biography of his friend:

> Constantly and everywhere, Batyushkov lived a life at odds with his vocation as a poet; wherever he was, in his short periods of leisure he poured out his feelings and thoughts . . . None of our poets has distinguished himself with such an amazing plenitude, such beautifully finished pictures as Batyushkov. He had the most complete

possession of his poetic inspiration and he was an artist in the full sense of the word. His poems are inimitable in their harmony, their truly Italian melody.

(WP, 238–39)

But Batyushkov warned him that this might be over-egging the cake, and in the end the first volume came out with a much more laconic foreword:

> These two little volumes include almost all Mr. Batyushkov's writings in prose and verse which are scattered through a range of periodicals, together with some new, unpublished works. I think it would be superfluous to discuss them in a preface. I shall simply say that having obtained the means of producing this edition, I consider it the most agreeable undertaking of my life, since I am sure that I shall satisfy the wishes of enlightened lovers of literature.

(Essays, 6)

The publication bore the modest title *Essays in Verse and Prose* (Opyty v stikhakh i proze). The word "essay" refers to Batyushkov's great French master, Montaigne, whose *Essais* are intended as attempts or trials, uncertain searchings rather than finished works. And indeed there is an epigraph from Montaigne at the head of the first volume: "Et quand personne ne me lira, ai-je perdu mon temps, de m'être entretenu tant d'heures oisives à pensements utiles ou agréables?" (And even if no one reads me, have I wasted my time in spending so many idle hours on useful or agreeable thoughts?). Like Montaigne, Batyushkov liked to refer to his works as "scribbling" or "trifles," but also, like Montaigne, he clearly attached more importance to them than he cared to admit.

For as he noted in the self-portrait quoted in the introduction, which was written in 1817 but not included in the *Essays*, he was very susceptible to the charms of fame. A good deal of his self-deprecating irony was part of a strategy of modesty designed to win praise. In the months preceding the publication of the *Essays,* his letters to Gnedich and others show him in a fever of self-doubt, fearing the exposure that awaits the published author. This comes across most clearly in a letter to Zhukovsky written from Khantonovo in June 1817:

> Why did I take it into my head to publish all this? I feel, I know, that there's a lot of rubbish here; even the poems that cost me so much torment me. But could it have been better? What a life I have led for poetry! Three wars, all the time on horseback or on the highways of the world. I ask myself: can you write anything perfect in such a stormy, changeable life? Conscience replies: No. Why publish then? It's no great disaster, of course; I'll be criticized and forgotten. But this thought kills me, it kills me, since I love fame and would like to deserve it, to tear it out of the hands of Fortune—not a great fame, no, just the little one that trifles can obtain for us if they are perfectly done ...
>
> *(SP, 408)*

And about his prose he wrote to Gnedich after rereading Montaigne: "There's a man! There's prose! And my stuff, I can see it myself, is thin gruel! It will all wither and soon fade. What's one to do! If the war hadn't ruined my health, I feel I could have written something better" (*SP*, 403). Not surprisingly, then, as work on the edition progressed, he was constantly seeking reassurance from his friends and bothering Gnedich with second thoughts, last-minute alterations, requests to leave out pieces that didn't pass muster. When success came, it must have been a relief.

Volume one, the prose, consists largely of pieces previously published in journals, many of them being the essays composed in Kamenets in 1815. Batyushkov worried that the collection might be a little slight, and suggested making a number of additions, only one of which was eventually included, a translation of "Griselda," the last story in Boccaccio's *Decameron*. He explained that he had translated freely, trying to capture something of the specific charm of the original. "Griselda" takes its place alongside essays on Tasso, Ariosto, and Petrarch; it is in fact the only survivor of Batyushkov's grandiose plan for a two-volume edition of translations of classic Italian texts and of important modern essays on Italian literature. He outlined this in a letter to Gnedich of March 1817, evidently hoping to enhance his reputation—and to make some money (*SP*, 403–5). But as with the translation of Tasso's epic, nothing came of it.

In volume two, devoted to poetry, there is a considerably greater proportion of new and unpublished writing. Although the opening poem, "To My Friends," presents the collection as a sort of poet's diary, a record of changing thoughts and feelings, Batyushkov decided against a chronological arrangement. The first and much the longest section is entitled "Elegies"—and Batyushkov is often seen as a crucial figure in establishing the elegy as the central poetic genre of the Russian Golden Age. The term is a capacious one in Russian literature, but essentially it is distinguished from the more formal ode by its concentration on the expression of personal feeling. Batyushkov's elegies are of many different kinds; few are as purely elegiac as "Shade of a Friend," and some (notably "Tasso Dying") are essentially historical narratives. It is important to note that in this section, translations (from Tibullus, Parny, and others) are intermingled with "original" poems; as we have seen, Batyushkov often worked by assimilating and re-creating poems from other languages, regarding the result as his own poetry.

The second section is devoted to "Epistles," though there are also epistles in "Elegies," notably the great poem addressed to Dashkov in 1813. The personal epistle was another field in which Batyushkov left a mark on the Russian poetry of his time, and this second section opens with what was perhaps his most famous poem, "My Penates." Then, after "Elegies" and "Epistles," comes the catchall "Miscellany," for the most part poems that are not spoken in the poet's name. Some of the pieces here might well have been placed in the earlier sections but arrived too late, when the rest of the volume had already been set up in print. The most important of these is "Tasso Dying," completed in the summer of 1817. Before it came such writings as "The Traveler and the Stay-at-Home," but also a variety of epigrams, inscriptions, and other short occasional pieces. What is not included, however, is the as yet unpublished "Vision on the Banks of Lethe." This had been a *succès de scandale* in manuscript, and friends urged Batyushkov to make it generally available, but he refused outright, not wishing to hurt poets he had satirized when he was younger. From the outset he made his position clear to Gnedich:

> I wouldn't print "Lethe" for a million rubles; I shall stand firm on this as long as I have a conscience, reason and a heart. Glinka is dying of hunger; Merzlyakov is a friend of mine, or what we call a friend; Shalikov is living in poverty; Yazykov is eating dust, and you want me to make a public laughingstock of them. No, I'd rather die!
>
> *(SP, 391–92)*

There were other poems, too, which he regretted having included in the *Essays*; he planned to remove them in a second edition—but this never materialized.

Meanwhile, he was composing new poems to fill out the second volume. In particular, he set himself to write a few more weighty pieces, for which he needed the isolation of Khantonovo. Most of these reached Gnedich too late to fit into the "Elegies" section where they really belong, the exception being a free translation of a poem by the French poet Millevoye, "The Rivalry of Hesiod and

Homer." Like "Tasso Dying," written soon after, this poem has a strongly personal theme, the conflictual relationship between the poet and society. Homer and Hesiod are shown competing in ceremonial games for the poet's prize; Homer sings of war and adventure, Hesiod of the beauty of the seasons. The weak king, more used to the pleasures of peacetime, "Scorned the lofty hymn of the immortal Homer / And awarded the palm to his rival." Hesiod is surrounded by enthusiastic crowds, while Homer flees the scene:

> Harassed by destiny right to the end,
> But still a king at heart, no slave to fate,
> Swallowing his grief in a deep wordlessness,
> Homer took flight from all the cares of court.
> And now a wretched Samian orphan boy
> Leads the blind bard from land to land, a son
> To him, but in Hellas they seek in vain—
> Talent and poverty never find a home.

> *(Essays, 248–49)*

We may remember that the life's work of Batyushkov's closest friend and editor was the translation of Homer's *Iliad*.

The second of these substantial poems, written in the winter of 1816–17, was "The Crossing of the Rhine," discussed in chapter 4. Here Batyushkov, far from the peaceful pleasures of his Epicurean verse, paints a battle scene with all the colorful expansiveness of a Homer. Immediately after this, almost at the end of the "Miscellany" section, and thus offering a grandiose conclusion to the *Essays*, is another long poem, the historical elegy "Tasso Dying." In letters to Gnedich and Zhukovsky, Batyushkov anxiously asks their opinion of this poem: "Did you like my 'Tasso'? I hope you did. I wrote it in the heat of the moment, with my mind full of all I had read about this great man" (*SP*, 407).

He had previously translated Torquato Tasso, had addressed a poem to him that prefigures this elegy, and was seen by friends as the Russian Tasso. Whether or not he had intimations of his own forthcoming collapse, he could identify with the Italian Renaissance poet who led a nomadic, tumultuous life, spending seven years in confinement with mental illness. At points Batyushkov's poem echoes the Romantic legend that Tasso's confinement was due to the jealousy and cruelty of the Duke of Ferrara. He writes in a long note that his "magnanimous protector shut him up in the hospital of Santa Anna—i.e. the madhouse—without trial or fault," and goes on to mention Montaigne's famous visit to the mad poet—"strange meeting in such a place of the foremost sage of modern times and the greatest poet!" There is no mistaking his personal involvement as he continues:

> To complete his misfortune, Tasso was not completely mad, and in moments of lucidity he felt all the bitterness of his confinement. Imagination, the principal source of his talent and his woes, never deserted him. Even in confinement he wrote unceasingly. At last, on the urgent request of all of Italy, and almost all of enlightened Europe, Tasso was freed (after a confinement of seven years, two months and a few days). But he did not enjoy his freedom for long. Somber memories, poverty, constant dependence on cruel people, the treachery of friends, the injustice of critics—in a word, all the griefs and misfortunes that can afflict a man, destroyed his strong constitution and brought him by a path of thorns to an early grave. Fortune, malicious to the end, reserved one final blow for him, scattering flowers on her victim. Pope Clement VIII, persuaded by the appeals of his nephew, Cardinal Cintio, and by the voice of all Italy, ordered a triumph for him on the Capitoline.
>
> (Essays, 331)

This is the point at which Batyushkov's poem begins, though the long speeches given to the dying poet carry the reader back over his whole life with references to his *Jerusalem Delivered* (La Gerusalemme liberata). The poem is one of his most formal, written in a high poetic style, with a sprinkling of archaic forms and expressions to create a solemn tone far removed from the playfulness of "My Penates." The meter is a Russian equivalent of the Greek elegiac couplet, with alternating masculine and feminine line endings. The epigraph from Tasso bewails the brevity of fame:

TASSO DYING

> . . . E come alpestre e rapido torrente,
> Come acceso baleno
> In notturno sereno,
> Come aura o fumo, o come stral repente,
> Volan le nostre fame; ed ogni orore
> Sembra languido fiore!
>
> Che più spera, o che s'attende omai?
> Dopo trionfo e palma
> Sol qui restano all'alma
> Lutto e lamenti, e lagrimosi lai.
> Che più giova amicizia o giova amore!
> Ahi lagrime! ahi dolore!
>
> *(Torquato Tasso, Torrismondo)*[3]

What festival is being made ready in old Rome?
Where are they bound, these floods of people?
Why this sweet-smelling smoke of spices and of myrrh,
These baskets full of aromatic grasses?

From Tiber's waters to the towering Capitol,
    Above the thronging universal city
Why have they hung these priceless rugs among
    The laurels, the flowers, the imperial purple?
And why this din, the thunder and the roar of drums,
    Is this a day of revelry or conquest?
Why does the vicar of Christ make his slow way
    Into the house of prayer with sacred banners?
And who will wear the garland in his trembling hands,
    The priceless present of a grateful city?
Whose triumph?—It is yours, who with your heavenly voice
    Sang of Jerusalem and liberation!
The noise of celebration carries to the cell
    Where Tasso is struggling with his final sickness
And where the spirit of death has stretched his wings
    Over the godlike forehead of the victim.
Neither the tears of friendship, nor the prayers of monks,
    Nor the honors heaped too late upon him,
Nothing can shield him from the iron hand of fate
    That knows no pity for our human greatness.
Already, half destroyed, he feels the lethal hour
    And welcomes it and calls it blessed,
With a sweet swan song once again, for the last time,
    He says farewell to life, exclaiming:

"O friends! let me once more look upon Rome the great
    Where an untimely grave awaits the poet.
Let my eyes rest upon your hills and on the smoke
    That rises from an ancient city's ashes.
O sacred land of heroes and of miracles!
    Eloquent dust of noble ruins!
Azure and purple richness of the cloudless skies

And poplar trees and venerable olives,
And you, eternal Tiber, where the peoples drank,
    Where bones of the world's citizens are scattered,
I greet you all, a captive of these cheerless walls,
    Condemned to die before my days are reckoned!

All is fulfilled! I stand above the dark abyss,
    And shall not hear the Capitol applauding;
Nor will fame's laurels sweeten the bitter taste
    That fills the air above my weary deathbed.
From my first days I was the people's laughingstock;
    When I was still a boy I lived in exile,
And like a poor vagabond all through Italy,
    Beneath its blessed skies I wandered.
What twists and turns of fate did I not suffer then?
    Where was my little boat not driven?
Where could I find a resting place? Where did my bread
    Not crumble in the tears of bitter sorrow?
Sorrento! Cradle of my unhappy days,
    Where in the depths of night, like sad Ascanius,
Destiny tore me from my mother's side,
    Her sweet embraces and her kisses,
As a boy you know how many tears I shed!
    Alas! since then, fate's constant victim,
I have known life's miseries, her bitterness,
    The fortune-furrowed waves lay open
Beneath me, and the thunder's voice was never hushed!
    Still driven from house to house, country to country,
I sought in vain the shelter of a port:
    Everywhere finding—her unrelenting finger!
Everywhere—thunderbolts to discipline the poet!
    And nowhere, not in the poor peasant's cottage,

Or safe from harm in Alonso's palace walls,
  Or in the quiet of some hidden dwelling,
In thickets or in hills, was there a place to lay
  My head, oppressed by fame or by its absence,
The head of a fugitive who from his earliest days
  Was the marked victim of the cruel goddess.

My friends! what is this weight that presses on my heart?
  Why does it shudder so? Why is it aching?
Where have I come from? What is the infernal road
  That I have traveled, what glimmers through the darkness?
Ferrara . . . Furies . . . and the envious hiss of snakes!
  Where shall I fly to, murderers of talent?
Rome is a place of refuge—place of brothers, friends,
  Their tears, the sweetness of their kisses . . .
And Virgil's laurel wreath, here in the Capitol!
  I have done everything that Phoebus ordered.
I was his zealous acolyte from my first youth,
  Harried by lightning and the wrath of heaven,
I sang the greatness and the fame of bygone days,
  And even in chains my soul did not betray him.
The Muses' heavenly fire was never quenched in me,
  In suffering my genius grew stronger.
It lived among the miracles, beneath the walls
  Of Zion, on the flowering banks of Jordan,
Haunting the peaceful havens of Lebanon,
  And questioning the Cedron's troubled waters.
Before my gaze you rose again, heroes of old,
  Exalted in your warlike stature.
I saw you, Godfrey, leader, overlord of kings,
  Calm, majestic in the hiss of arrows;
And you, Rinaldo, like Achilles in the fight,

Heaven-favored conqueror in love and battle,
I saw you flying over bodies, once your foes,
　　Like fire, like death, exterminating angel . . .
And Tartarus was laid low beneath the shining cross.
　　O paragons of valor without equal!
O holy triumph of our distant ancestors
　　Now gone to endless sleep! Pure faith triumphant!
Torquato rescued you from the deep chasm of time:
　　He sang—and you will never be forgotten—
He sang and won the crown of immortality
　　Woven by fame and by the seven Muses.
It is too late. I stand above the dark abyss,
　　And shall not see the applauding Capitol;
Nor will fame's laurels sweeten the bitter taste
　　That fills the air above my weary deathbed."

He said no more. His eyes burned with a dusky flame,
　　The last gleam of a dying poet's spirit,
As if he hoped to snatch out of the hand of Fate
　　A day of triumph in his final moments.
His gaze still searching for the Capitol,
　　He tried in vain to rouse his dying body;
But, worn out by the fearful agony of death,
　　Could only lie stretched on his bed, unmoving.
The sun was gliding westward to its resting place
　　And sinking in a glow of crimson;
The hour of death drew closer . . . now for the last time
　　A light shone from his somber features.
With a tranquil smile he looked out to the west
　　And animated by the cool of evening,
He raised his right hand to the watchful heavens
　　Like a righteous man who speaks of hope and comfort,

And said to his grieving friends: "Look there, how in the west
    The sun, greatest of all the lights, is blazing!
He calls on me to follow him to cloudless lands,
    Where the eternal Light will rise upon me . . .
Already an angel stands before me as my guide
    And overshadows me with wings of azure . . .
Bring me the sign of love, the sacramental cross,
    And pray with hope and tears of supplication . . .
All earthly things can only die—fame, laurel wreaths . . .
    The mighty works of art and of the muses:
But there all is eternal, like the eternal God
    Who gives the crown of never-failing glory!
There, there is all the greatness that inspired my soul,
    All I have lived for since the cradle.
O brothers, friends, you must not shed your tears for me,
    Your friend has won the treasure that he longed for.
He will go from this world, and given strength by faith,
    He will not feel the terror of his passing:
There, there . . . o joy! among the uncorrupted souls
    Among the angels Eleonora will meet him!"

Speaking of love, the heavenly poet breathed his last;
    His friends stood weeping over him in silence.
The day burned slowly out, a bell's transparent voice
    Carried the sorry tidings to the city.
"Torquato our poet is dead!" a weeping Rome exclaimed,
    "The bard is dead, he deserved a kinder fortune! . . ."
The next day they beheld the torches' somber smoke,
    And the Capitoline was draped in mourning.

(Essays, 325–30)

Batyushkov concluded his note on the poem with the words: "May the shade of the great poet not be offended that a son of the gloomy north, who owes to the *Gerusalemme liberata* the best and sweetest moments of his life, has ventured to bring this meager handful of flowers to his memory!" In fact, he thought the poem the best he had written, and originally wanted it to begin the volume, in place of an author's portrait. Contemporaries saw in it a reflection of the poet's own tribulations, especially after his mental collapse, and most thought highly of it. It does not actually conclude the *Essays*, being followed by a happier and less grandiloquent poem written in the summer of 1817; this celebration of the construction of a summerhouse strikes once more some of the chords of Batyushkov's earlier epistles to friends, the praise of country solitude, the pleasure in poetry:

THE MUSES' ARBOR

Here, under the bird-cherry's creamy shade,
    Beneath the acacias' golden beauty,
I build an altar to the blessed muses,
    Companions of my younger days.

I bring them flowers, the amber of the bees,
    And the first fruits of the meadow,
And may my humble presents bring them pleasure,
    My grateful song beneath the trees!

The poet does not pray to them for gold;
    They have no time for riches;
They are the allies of the poor and needy,
    In huts, not palaces, at home.

He does not pray for fame's resplendent gifts;
　　Alas! his voice is feeble.
A bee can never, like the mighty eagle,
　　Soar boldly to the heights.

He prays the muses that they will return
　　To his tired soul the love of beauty,
And the bright cheerfulness that used to burn,
　　And freshness to his flagging feelings.

And may care with its heavy load
　　Drown in the river of oblivion,
And greedy time not touch the muses' favorite
　　In this, his calm abode.

May he, no longer young, but young in heart,
　　The carefree child of the carefree graces,
Sometimes come here to rest in the deep shade
　　Of the bird-cherries and acacias.

(*Essays, 333–34*)

Two more poems were completed just before the publication of the *Essays*. The first is another verse epistle; it is addressed to Batyushkov's cousin Nikita, a close friend and the son of his former protector Mikhail Muravyov. Nikita was more than ten years his junior, but the two had both fought in the Napoleonic wars. In 1812, at the age of fifteen, Nikita had run away from home to join the army; to his regret, however, he had not had the thrill of riding into Paris with the Russian army. In his earlier writings and letters, Batyushkov often spoke of the tonic effect of military life on his lethargic and depressive nature; here, finding common ground with his young cousin, he recalls one last time the glory days of wartime and contrasts them with the dull and forgotten existence he lives in Khantonovo. Vivid passages in his realistic description of military life anticipate much later writing by Lermontov, in particular his long poem "Valerik."[4]

TO NIKITA

Comrade in arms, I love to see
Spring bursting out in gay abundance,
And then for the first time to hear
The lark's bright song above the meadow.
But it's sweeter far to see the fields
Coming alive with tents and banners
And to lie carefree by the fires
Waiting for daybreak and the battle.
What happiness, my gallant knight,
To gaze down from a hillside lookout
At the green valleys stretching bright
Beneath the endless ranks of soldiers!
How sweet to hear outside the tent
The far-off roar of cannon at evening
And sink ourselves deep into sleep
Beneath our greatcoats till the morning,
When we shall hear in the dewy sun
The early horses' trot and clatter
And the long-drawn-out growl of guns
Stirring the echoes on the mountains.
What joy it is to race along
The ranks of soldiers on your charger,
And plunge the first into the throng,
Shouting and slashing with your saber!
What joy to hear the order: "Charge!

Infantry, cossacks!—Charge, hussars!
After the enemy, chasseurs!—
Highlanders, Bashkirs, Tatars!"
Whistle and buzz, bullets of lead!
Grapeshot and shells, come flying over!
What do they care for you, our men
Made for the battlefield by nature?
Like a forest the columns move . . .
O what a glorious sight!—none better!
They march—their silence speaks of war;
They march—their muskets at the ready;
They march . . . Hurrah! It's all knocked out,
Everything scattered in the rout.
Hurrah! Where are the enemy?
They've run away. We're in their quarters.
O happy warriors!—and now we
Drink captured wine from shining helmets
And as victorious cannons roar,
Sing a *Te Deum* to the Lord . . .

But you are trembling eagerly,
Clutching your saber, my young warrior.
Your soul is troubled, and I see
You long to go and pluck the laurel.
On the bloody battlefield
You with the spirit of Suvorov
Go wandering, but cannot find
In this weak world a worthy fortune.
But never fear—when the thunder roars,
You'll hasten to the flags of honor,
But there, alas! you'll see no more
Your friend among the eager soldiers.

Forgotten by vociferous fame,
That sweet tormentor of the spirit,
I sleep here, like a weary peasant
Who never hears the voice of praise.

(Essays, 303–4)

The poem was meant as a surprise to the twenty-year-old Nikita; Batyushkov specifically asked Gnedich not to show it to him until the book came out, adding ruefully: "That's the sort of trifles that I busy myself with, thirty-year-old child that I am" (*WP*, 243). He gave his *Essays* to Nikita with a heartfelt dedication, but the young man, whatever he may have thought of the epistle, was not impressed by the conservative aspect of the prose pieces, and wrote unflattering notes in the margins of his copy (see *Works, 26–29*). For although the cousins were very close at this time and both members of Arzamas, their political views were some way apart. Nikita Muravyov was one of the early members of what became the insurrectionary Decembrist movement. Though he did not actually take part in the uprising of December 1825, he was found guilty of conspiracy and condemned to death, this being commuted to twenty years of hard labor. Batyushkov, on the other hand, while he was close to several of the future Decembrists, had little sympathy with their aims; he had satirized the literary conservatives around Admiral Shishkov, but turned away from what he came to regard as the destructive ideas of the French Enlightenment, preferring the more accepting wisdom of Montaigne.

Finally, let us return to the poem Batyushkov first wrote at the age of fifteen, "Dreaming," already briefly discussed in chapter 1. Though this poem is hardly on a level with his best writing, it clearly mattered a great deal to him, and he placed the final, rewritten and much expanded version at the end of the "Elegies" section of the *Essays;* easily the longest of the elegies, this hymn to imagination seems thus to proclaim the poet's enduring artistic credo. Much of the expansion consists of lengthy developments of the Nordic/ Ossianic and the Anacreontic/erotic motifs; the poem then concludes very much like the first version—echoing in 1817 the sentiments with which Batyushkov began it in 1802:

> You, Dream, be true to me, and live with me!
> Society, the empty gleam of fame
> Can never take the place of what you give!
> Let fools prize glittering vanity,
> Kissing the golden dust of marble halls—
> But I am rich and happy when I have
> Found for myself repose and freedom,
> Leaving society's worries to oblivion!
> And may I never forget
> The poet's happy lot: to know
> In poetry the happiness of Dream!
> The smallest thing delights him; as a bee
> Weighed down with golden pollen
> Buzzes from grass to flowers
> And thinks a stream the sea,
> The poet sees a palace in his retreat—
> Happy because *he dreams.*

(Essays, 259)

In spite of Batyushkov's fears, the publication of the *Essays* was a great success. Like many writers of the time, he had published widely in journals, and together with his manuscript writings (notably the "Vision on the Banks of Lethe") these had already given him a considerable reputation. But the appearance of two volumes of prose and verse, including many new works, made it clear that here was one of the outstanding poets of the age. Batyushkov was no doubt reassured, at least for the time being. Even four years later, when he was convinced that the world was against him, he remembered the high point of his career: "Then all the journalists, without a single exception, showered me with praise, undeserved no doubt, but praise" (*SP*, 441). However badly things were to go subsequently, the *Essays* of 1817 had established him as a major Russian writer.

TO ITALY

After the publication of the *Essays*, Batyushkov wrote very little else, or at least very little that has survived. Later on, he described his subsequent "silence" as deliberate, but this seems unlikely, the more so in that it was not complete. Indeed he had many ideas for writing, and did in fact produce some of his most memorable work in these years, notably the brief and brilliant poems translated from or inspired by the lyrics of the Greek Anthology.

Once he had more or less finished work on the *Essays*, at Khantonovo in May 1817, he wrote down some thoughts in a notebook. He kept notebooks at other times, but apart from this one, the only comparable texts to have survived are some reading notes of 1810 (discussed in chapter 3). Many of the jottings of 1817 are also reactions to books read; indeed, they are given the title "Other People's Stuff is My Treasure"—a form of words that points up the close links of reading and writing for Batyushkov and his contemporaries. But there are also notes that give a more direct insight into his inner world. The first of these reads:

> I must never lose the beautiful passion for the *beautiful*, which so attracts one to the arts and literature, but I must not become surfeited with it. Moderation in all things. The works of Racine, Tasso,

Virgil and Ariosto can captivate a fresh soul: happy the man who at thirty can weep, can shed tears of emotion. Horace asked that Zeus should end his life when he became *impervious to the sounds of the lyre.* I very much understand this prayer . . .

(Essays, 410)

This sounds a note that we often hear in his letters to friends: the weariness that makes it difficult for him to maintain old enthusiasms, to settle anywhere, or indeed to write. He continues, a little later, with a fascinating account of his attempts to deal with this:

My illness hasn't gone away, but it has calmed down a bit. All around me is a gloomy silence, the house is empty, it's drizzling, the garden is muddy. What can I do? I've read all there was, even the *European Herald.* Let me recall the old days. Let me write spontaneously, impromptu, without narcissism, and see what comes pouring out—write as fast as you speak, with no ulterior motive, the way few people write, since narcissism is always plucking at your sleeve and getting you to put a different word in place of the one you first thought of. But Montaigne wrote whatever came into his mind. True. But Montaigne is a quite exceptional man. I compare his mind to a spring that has been dammed up—open the sluice and the water comes rushing out, endlessly flowing, foaming and boiling, always clear and healthy—and why? Because there was a great reservoir of water. With a small mind, a weak or sluggish one, like mine, it's very hard to write spontaneously, but today I'm in the mood, I want to perform a *tour de force.* My pen will dispel my melancholy a little. So then . . . But I'm stuck already. How to begin? What to write about? Recall the past, describe the present, plan for the future. But you have to admit that's all very tedious. Speaking of the past is all right when you're old and very important or rich, talking to your heirs, who listen out of kindness: "On en vaut mieux quand on est écouté."[1] What can you say about the present? It hardly exists. And the future? . . . ah, the future's been very burdensome to me recently! So then, write about something: discuss something! I've tried discussing things, but it never seems to work; when I discuss something—as kind people tell me—it's like when other people show off. That's a painful thought. Why can't I discuss things?

And he goes into a comic routine, listing eleven reasons (such as his short stature) for his inability to think, then carries on:

But I must write. I'm bored without a pen in hand. I've tried drawing, but it's no good; what shall I do? help me, good people—but I've no one to talk to. I don't know how to cope with my misery. Let's see. As it happens, I recall someone's words—Voltaire's, I remember now: "Et voilà comme on écrit l'histoire!"[2] These words came back automatically, I don't know why, and they set me off remembering events I have witnessed in my life and what I have subsequently read in descriptions of these events. What a difference, my God, what a difference! "Et voilà comme on écrit l'histoire."

And he is off, telling stories of his wartime commander Raevsky and the gap between what actually happened and the legends that grew up around it, then moving on to a brief portrait of the general, "a great warrior and sometimes a good man, sometimes a very strange one." And he concludes: "I've written all that without flagging. God be praised! An hour has flown past without my noticing it" (*Essays*, 410–16). Getting through the days could be a burden.

Batyushkov did have ideas for further writing. We have seen in the previous chapter his plans for a long poem on a theme from Russian folklore ("Rusalka") and for a collection of translations from the Italian. The notebook of 1817 adds an unexpectedly ambitious outline for an "agreeable and useful book," a very full history of

Russian literature designed for a society readership who knew their own literature less well than those of Western Europe. Batyushkov had written earlier to Gnedich of his problems with the Russian language, but now, in the aftermath of the Napoleonic wars, he is pursuing the patriotic agenda he had suggested in "An Evening at Kantemir's." It is not clear whether he had any intention of embarking on this venture himself, but he develops his scheme in some detail, starting with the old Slavonic language and the literature of the Middle Ages, but devoting the vast majority of the volume to post-Petrine writing. He lists a huge range of writers, including his contemporaries, under twenty-eight different headings, and suggests a number of topical themes and questions:

> The influence of the newborn German literature—and in part that of English literature. What have we achieved? Why has the lyrical genre [i.e. the ode] flourished and why must it decline? What is most characteristically Russian? The richness and poverty of the language. Can a language thrive without a philosophy, and why can it thrive, but not for long? The influence of church language on that of civil society, and the influence of civil eloquence on spiritual eloquence . . .
>
> (*Essays, 422*)

It could have been a fascinating and timely book, but none of it was ever written.

Another aspect of this notebook is the new concern for morality that we saw also in the essays of 1815. It is here that we find the remarkable double self-portrait that is cited at length in the introduction. Batyushkov's key value in these notes seems to be *sniskhozhdenie*, which can be translated as tolerance or indulgence. He sees this—somewhat contrary to his earlier satirical practice— as an essential value in literary life:

From whatever angle you look at man in himself and in society, you find that tolerance must be the first of virtues. Tolerance in speech, in deed, and in thought—that is what gives an attractiveness to goodness, which is almost more appealing than anything in the world. To frown and pick up Juvenal's big stick is not very difficult, but to jest with life, like Horace, that's the true philosopher's stone . . .

Simplicity and tolerance are the signs of a mind made for art . . . The Savior's words on the poor in spirit who inherit the kingdom of heaven can be applied to the literary world too.

(Essays, 418, 428)

This expresses the thirty-year-old poet's new outlook, more Christian, more quietist, more conservative. It tended to separate him from his younger, more radical, more combative friends, those who would go on to form the Decembrist conspiracy against the autocracy that the poet was content to serve.

And indeed government service of some kind was becoming a pressing need for Batyushkov in 1817. His finances, already shaky, were dealt a further blow when his father died in November, leaving Konstantin as head of the family, responsible for paying his father's debts and looking after his siblings, including two children of his father's second marriage. He didn't attempt to duck these responsibilities, taking out new loans and selling off some of his own property to prevent the sale of his father's house. In particular his letters show his extreme concern for the welfare and education of his little half brother Pompey, born in 1811, who was to help with the edition of his works seventy years later. His income was barely adequate for all this. The success of the *Essays* brought in little money. In the light of his newfound fame, he was made an honorary librarian of the Imperial Public Library where he had served as a younger man—this gave him honor, but not cash. Consequently, he kept coming back to his old plan of obtaining a diplomatic post in his poetic homeland, Italy. As well as cultural riches, this would have the advantage of a warmer climate, which he found himself needing more and more as his various ailments continued to harass him. In June 1817, he had written to Zhukovsky: "Winter is the death of me. Even when I was quite healthy, I froze like a cabbage-stalk in France . . . imagine what it's like for me here in Russia, with our killing frosts! Let's go to the Crimea, 'wo die Zitronen blühn'" (*SP*, 409).[3]

In fact, the following summer he went nearly as far as the Crimea, bathing assiduously in the sea at Odessa, while fulfilling his role as honorary librarian by studying the antiquities of southern Russia. But Italy was the real dream. In June 1818, on the persuasion—and with the help—of Zhukovsky and other friends, he plucked up his courage and submitted his case in a letter to the tsar. Describing his life, his campaigns, and his illnesses, he wrote of his desire to use his modest knowledge and abilities for the good of the Fatherland, while profiting from a climate "necessary for the restoration of my health which was shattered by my wound and the hardships of the Finnish campaign" (*WP*, 260–61). The following month he received an appointment to the Russian mission in Naples, with a modest salary.

■ □ ■

Meanwhile he had continued to play his part in the literary life of the capital. As already noted, his *Essays in Verse and in Prose* were received with great acclaim, and no dissenting voices, in the autumn of 1817—Batyushkov must have felt at least partly reassured by this success. Arriving in St. Petersburg not long before publication, he was at long last able to attend meetings of Arzamas. In fact, by this time the society was beginning to change—but also to decline and disperse. Since Derzhavin's death in 1816, Arzamas's old adversary, the Circle of Lovers of the Russian Word, was no longer active, so there was no obvious literary fight to be fought. Some members were departing from St. Petersburg—Zhukovsky to Moscow, Vyazemsky to Warsaw, others on foreign missions. At the same time, new members were seeking to inflect it more toward radical politics. In order to breathe new life into Arzamas, there was a proposal to found a new literary-political journal. In the end nothing came of this, but Batyushkov did produce one outstanding contribution, which was later published separately (and semi-anonymously). This is a group of translations of poems from the Greek Anthology, the famous collection of several thousand short Greek poems by a great variety of authors from the seventh-century BCE to the tenth-century CE.

Batyushkov knew no Greek, and the translations were done from French versions of the Greek produced by his Arzamas colleague Sergey Uvarov, a classical scholar who later played an important educational role in the reactionary government of Nicholas I. Indeed, Batyushkov's poems were intended originally to provide illustrations for Uvarov's article on the Anthology. They are for the most part love poems, a lot of them in the erotic mode that Batyushkov had earlier found in Parny. In many of them, love is threatened, and one or two, including the first one (taken from Meleager), are poems of loss and mourning. The very short final piece strikes a different note, celebrating courage in the face of death. In all cases, though, there is a memorable concision, a striking richness of imagery, a beauty of orchestration and a fluidity of construction characteristic of their author. As usual with his translations, they show a freedom that allows the poet to express his own vision and his own feelings, in his own voice. The meter is a characteristically Russian iambic, with lines of varying length, and there are irregular rhyme schemes mixing masculine and feminine endings (though my translations are largely unrhymed). Here is the full collection of thirteen poems:

FROM THE GREEK ANTHOLOGY

I

In nothingness's gloomy mansion
O woman unforgettable! accept from me
Tears and despairing cries on your cold tombstone,
   Roses ephemeral as you!
   All is in vain. Eternal darkness
Will not give up your ever-grieving shadow;
We cannot call you back from envious Hades.
Here all is dumb and cold; here nothing speaks.
My funeral torch only reveals the blackness . . .
What have you done, you governors of heaven?
Say, why does beauty have so short a life?
But mother earth, take these my bitter tears,
Take her who sleeps, the faded flower of spring,
And may she rest in hospitable shade.

II

Witnesses of my love and sorrow,
Youthful roses, damp with tears!
Deck with your wreaths the modest cottage
Where my beloved shuns our eyes.
Remain, sweet wreaths, and do not wither!
But if she comes, pour out on her
All your sweet odor, and once more
Water with tears her lovely tresses.
May she stand wondering, and sigh;

And you, flowers, with your fragrant breath,
Water with tears my dear one's tresses.

III

At last! Nikagor and fire-breathing Eros
With Bacchus' cups have vanquished Aglaya . . .
O joy, that here they have unloosed the girdle,
Once the proud bulwark of her maidenhood!
See all around the room carelessly scattered
The gorgeous clothing of disdainful beauty,
The floating vestments of light, snowy gauze,
The shapely shoes, the flowers freshly picked.
All these, the ruins of her rich apparel,
Proclaim her love, Nikagor's happiness.

IV

THE SYCAMORE TO THE PASSERBY

See how the vine entwines me in its tendrils!
See how it loves my half-decaying trunk!
Once I cast over it a grateful shadow;
Now I have withered . . . but the vine stays true.
       So pray to Zeus,
If you are made for friendship, passerby,
That your friend too will one day be like mine
And love your dust while he remains alive.

V

Where is the fame, the beauty that undid you?
The busy streets, the happy citizens?
Where are the sumptuous halls, the noble temples,
The gold, the tessera that shone in them?
Alas, great many-pillared Corinth, gone forever,
Your very ash is scattered through the fields,
All is a void, we only cry to heaven,
The halcyon alone grieves in the mist!

VI

"Where are you going, my beauty?—Business, none of yours.
—And can I hope?—For what?—You know quite well.
—I haven't time!—But look here, count this gold.
—And is that all? You're joking! So, farewell."

VII

Let's hide forever from men's envious eyes
The ardent raptures and the swoon of passion.
How sweet a kiss in the unspeaking night,
How sweet love's hidden pleasures!

VIII

I love the smile playing on Laisa's lips,
Her talk that captivates the heart, but dearer

Than everything to me are her shy looks
And in her eyes the tears of sudden sorrow.
Last night at twilight, overcome by passion,
I knelt again before her, spoke of love:
    My kisses led her on to pleasure
    On the soft couch laid out for us . . .
    I burned with love, she stood unmoving . . .
    But suddenly grew pale, despondent
    And tears came flooding from her eyes!
Taken aback, I pressed her to my bosom:
"What's troubling you, my dear, what's troubling you?"
"Don't worry, it is nothing, God's my witness;
    Just one thought troubles me," she said:
"You men are faithless, and . . . I feel afraid."

IX

Is it for you to mourn your young days gone?
    You are as beautiful as ever
And with the passing years
Ever more captivating to your lover.
I do not prize an inexperienced beauty,
Unskilled in all the mysteries of love;
Her bashful gaze is lifeless and unspeaking,
Her timid kisses by no feeling moved.
    But you, love's empress, could awaken
    An answering passion in a stone
And in your autumn days the flame still burns
    That through your bloodstream flows.

X

Alas! these eyes bedimmed by weeping,
The hours of suffering in these hollow cheeks,
They don't awaken your compassion—
A cruel smile plays on your lips . . .
These are the bitter fruits of passion,
Sad fruits of passion that no joy relieves,
The fruits of love, worthy of favor
And not the fate that so benumbs the heart . . .
Alas! like sudden lightning up in heaven,
Passions eat up our early years,
Perfidiously, they leave us cheerless,
Afflicted by never-ending tears.
But you, my beauty, you whose love is dearer
To me than all my youth and happiness,
Take pity on me . . . and I will recover,
Younger and brighter than I was.

XI

An eloquent look, a passionate smile,
Which, like a mirror show the soul
Of my beloved . . . She
By a harsh Argus is kept away from me!
But passion's eyes can see through walls:
You jealous man, beware the love in eyes!
Love showed me the mysteries of happiness,
Love will show me the way to my beloved,
Love did not teach you how to read our hearts.

XII

Life is exhausted in my frozen heart:
An end to struggle and to everything!
Eros and Aphrodite, you tormentors,
Hear my last words, my melancholy!
I fade away, yet undergo new tortures,
        Half dead, but not consumed,
I fade away, my love is still as ardent,
        And without hope I die!
So on the altar, round the sacrifice,
        The fire grows pale and dwindles,
Then, flaring up before it dies,
        Is quenched amid the ashes.

XIII

With courage in my looks, fire burning in my blood,
I sailed, but suddenly cruel death stormed the horizon.
Young sailor, don't forget how beautiful your life is!
        Trust to your boat! Sail on the flood!

(Essays, 344–48)

Together with their even more striking sequel, *Imitations of the Ancients*, these poems are a high point in Batyushkov's writing and quickly came to be seen as a major contribution to Russian poetry, establishing a new genre, the "anthological poem."[4] Batyushkov was only identified by his Arzamas initial (A for Achilles) in the first publication, but his young contemporary Wilhelm Küchelbecker wrote that from the delight felt in reading them, from their beautiful melody, the skill of the translation and the perfection of the prosody, they could only be the work of Batyushkov or Aleksandr Pushkin— but more probably the former (*WP*, 258).

■ □ ■

In the late summer of 1818, having learned of his appointment to Naples, Batyushkov returned to St. Petersburg. Soon after his arrival he sent to the wife of the historian Karamzin a little poem in praise of her husband's work. The eighth volume of his *History of the Russian State* had appeared earlier that year, and Batyushkov, who had always admired and loved Karamzin, was distressed that it was receiving too little attention; to make up for this, in a typically self-deprecating way, he composed these "poor lines." "They just poured out from my soul," he wrote to Aleksandr Turgenev:

> *TO THE AUTHOR OF THE HISTORY*
> *OF THE RUSSIAN STATE*
> _____
>
> When once at the Olympic Games,
> In hopes of sweet applause, the father
> Of history pronounced the names
> Of Greeks who crushed the kings of Asia
> And shattered all their proud batallions,
> The people, all athirst for glory,
> Forgot their games and entertainments
> And stood enraptured by his story.
> But in the midst of the great crowd
> The noble young Thucidydes,
> Beloved of the muses, stood
> And drank the old historian's words.

How thirstily he then would listen
To the old tales of mighty warriors,
And how he wept, what joyful tears
Came running down his burning cheeks!
So I too wept in exultation
On reading your immortal words
And blessed your genius, sweetly stirred
With irresistible emotion.
What if I have no gift, no talent!—
The muses spoke to me of art,
Beauty could move me, I was able
To feel your genius in my heart.

(*CP, 233–34*)

Meanwhile he was preparing himself for his posting to Naples. It was what he had long wanted, yet he was far from overjoyed at the prospect of leaving Russia and his friends. In September he wrote an occasional poem of thanks to Prince Shalikov (a poet whose work he had previously scorned in private letters), speaking of the new life that awaited him and of his intention of giving up the literary life:

I shall leave my fathers' place for a new world,
A new sky and new faces far from home,
Vesuvius on fire, Etna's eternal pall,
Castrati, opera, clowns, the Pope in Rome,
The sacred dust of the world's capital.
But everywhere (or so I say on my good days)
My soul will be the same, I shall stay true,
        I shall remember when I die
Moscow, the fatherland, my friends, and you!

(*CP, 235*)

A similar attachment to his Russian friends is expressed in a gloomy and prophetic letter sent on September 10 to Turgenev, who had worked hard to get him this posting:

> I know Italy without having been there. I shan't find happiness there: it doesn't exist anywhere. I'm even certain that I shall feel homesick for the snows of home and the people who are so dear to me. Neither the magnificent spectacle of nature, nor the wonders of art, nor the grandiose memories will make up for you and the friends whom I have *got used* to loving. Got used! Do you understand me? But the first thing is to live, and it's cold here, and I am dying daily. That's why I desired and still desire Italy.

In spite of misgivings, he set out. On November 19, he was given a champagne send-off from Tsarskoe Selo by a great company of writers, including Gnedich, Zhukovsky, and the young Pushkin. He traveled first to Vienna, from where he sent a miserable letter to his aunt Muravyova: "I dare not say what I was thinking on the second and third day after my departure, but these days were the saddest of my life and I shall remember them a long, long time" (*CP*, 11). But by January 1819 he was in Rome, and apparently more cheerful, writing to Olenin: "One stroll in Rome, one glance at the Forum (with which I am totally in love), are more than enough to repay me for all the discomforts of my journey" (*SP*, 425).

He was to stay in Rome for a few weeks, devouring the sights, and seeing a good deal of the young Russian artists who had received grants from the Russian Academy of Arts to study there. Since Batyushkov's protector Olenin was responsible for this scheme, he had given the poet the task of checking on the grant-holders and reporting on their work. He went beyond this commission to argue for improving their conditions (which were much inferior to those of their French equivalents). He also struck up a particular friendship with the landscape painter Silvestr Shchedrin, who had been in Italy for some months and who later came to stay with him in Naples.

The Naples stay lasted nearly two years, from March 1819 to the end of 1820. These were crucial years in Batyushkov's life, coming after the success of the *Essays* and preceding his collapse into madness, but we have very little information about them—only a few letters, three short poems, and occasional mentions in other people's letters and memoirs. No doubt there were many more letters, since correspondence with friends at home was a lifeline; in August 1819 he wrote to Zhukovsky: "I begin this letter as usual with reproaches that you have completely forgotten me, dear friend. I am constantly writing to Turgenev, writing to everyone, occasionally (very rarely) I get a reply, but to my annoyance not a line from you . . . The day when I receive a letter from Russia is the best of all days for me" (*SP*, 436). In the same letter he notes: "I am quite unable to write verse," but adds that he is writing assiduously in prose, "notes on the antiquities around Naples." All this prose has disappeared, perhaps burned by Batyushkov together with poems and other material in 1822.

A major disappointment in Italy was his failure to recover his health. He complains:

> Unfortunately, and I can't speak of this without a feeling of indignation, my health is constantly declining: neither the sun, nor the mineral waters, nor the strictest diet have been able to put it right; it seems to have been irretrievably destroyed. My chest too, which until now only rarely troubled me, has completely failed. Italy is no help to me; I'm freezing here, what would I be like in the north? I daren't think about going home.
>
> (*SP, 438*)

Nevertheless, he was well enough at times to respond enthusiastically to the life and natural scenes surrounding him. The letter from which I have just quoted was written from the island of Ischia in August 1819 and contains an eloquent description of "the most magnificent sight in the world"—the whole stretch of the Bay of Naples from Sorrento to the hills near Rome—and of the amazing brightness of the starry sky and the Milky Way. The previous March, not long after his arrival, he painted for Turgenev a dramatic picture of the contrasts of life in Naples:

> Every day the people flood into the immense theatre to go into raptures over the music of Rossini and the mellifluous singing of their sirens, while at the same time our neighbor Vesuvius is preparing to erupt; they say that in Portici [near Herculaneum] and places nearby the wells are beginning to go dry—a sign, according to the observers, that the volcano is about to go into action. What an amazing country! Here there are earthquakes, floods, eruptions with burning lava and ash, there are also fires, epidemics and fevers. Whole mountains disappear and mountains emerge from the sea; others suddenly begin to breathe fire. Here the marshes or the exhalations from the earth infect the volcanic air and give birth to contagions: people die like flies. But on the other hand, here there is eternal, blazing sunshine, quiet and gentle moonlight, and the very air which contains death is sweet and perfumed! Everything has its good side. Pliny died in the ashfall, his nephew describes his death. On the ash grow sweet grapes and luscious vegetables.
>
> (SP, 430–31)

In many respects, Batyushkov warmed to his new surroundings, but the beauty and interest of Naples could not overcome his sadness and longing for home: "By day it is fun to wander along the seafront in the shade of flowering pomegranates, but in the evening it's not a bad thing to sit with friends round a good fire and have a good talk" (SP, 432). He felt lost without the company of such bosom companions as Gnedich and Zhukovsky. He had no great success in his contact with local people, and the Russian company was limited. What made matters worse was his situation in the Russian mission, where he found himself at odds with his superior, Count Gustav Ernst Stackelberg, an experienced diplomat who liked to throw his weight around. According to one of Batyushkov's close friends, when he disagreed with a paper he had been given to copy, Stackelberg cut him off, saying: "You're not here to discuss things" (*WP*, 279). Such treatment pushed him inward, into greater isolation, hypochondria, and actual illness. Nor was he roused from his lethargy by the revolution of the *carbonari* in the summer of 1820—in its way a prefiguration of the Decembrist uprising in which several of Batyushkov's young friends would be involved. His only reaction, as far as we know, was a note to his aunt saying: "I'm really fed up with this stupid revolution. It's time to be sensible, in other words, be quiet" (*WP*, 282).

Nevertheless, even if he felt incapable of writing poetry, the Naples period did produce at least three remarkable short pieces (more may well be lost). The first was triggered by a visit to Baia (in antiquity, Baiae), a fashionable seaside resort for the rich in Roman times, whose ruins were largely submerged by volcanic activity. Batyushkov responded with intense nostalgia for a lost world. His beautifully shaped piece is one of his most perfect creations; it was not published until 1857, two years after his death:

> You wake, o Baiae, from the tomb
> With the first coming of Aurora's rays,
> But rosy dawn will not return to you
>   The radiance of vanished days.
> She will not bring again the cool retreats
>   Where swarms of beauties played,
> And never will your porphyry colonnades
>   Rise from the depth of the blue waves.

(Essays, 348)

The second poem, written a month or two later, is, like many of Batyushkov's poems, a free translation. He knew little English, but on Ischia in August 1819 he came across an Italian translation of the fourth canto of Byron's *Childe Harold*, which was first published in English the previous year. This was the period when Byron's fame was sweeping through Europe; as Aleksandr Turgenev noted, Zhukovsky was dreaming of him in St. Petersburg and Vyazemsky was enthusiastic about him in Prague while the Italians were translating him. But the first Russian verse translation of Byron appears to be that of Batyushkov, whose version echoes in some respects his poems from the Greek Anthology. He started from the following lines (Canto IV, stanzas 178–79):

> There is a pleasure in the pathless woods,
> There is a rapture on the lonely shore,
> There is society, where none intrudes,
> By the deep Sea, and music in its roar:
> I love not Man the less, but Nature more,
> From these our interviews, in which I steal
> From all I may be, or have been before,
> To mingle with the Universe and feel
> What I can ne'er express, yet cannot all conceal.
>
> Roll on, thou deep and dark blue ocean—roll!
> Ten thousand fleets sweep over thee in vain;
> Man marks the earth with ruin—his control
> Stops with the shore . . .

What in Byron is a personal digression at the end of a long narrative becomes a freestanding lyric poem in which the romantic appeal of nature to the disillusioned man is heightened. The translation is quite close, closer than in many of Batyushkov's earlier versions of

Parny, Tibullus, and others, but Byron's stanzaic form is replaced by the elegiac couplets that Batyushkov often favored. It seems strange to "retranslate" Byron back into English from a Russian text, itself based on an Italian translation of the English, but this will give an idea of Batyushkov's poem:

> There is delight too in the forests' wildness,
> > And gladness on the ocean's shore,
> Harmony in the sound of breakers
> > Exploding in their rush and roar.
> I love my neighbor, but you, nature,
> > Are dearer than all things to the heart!
> With you, my sovereign, I no more remember
> > The man I was, and I forget
> What I am now in my decrepitude.
> > In you my feelings live again:
> I cannot put them into shapely words,
> > Yet how can I not speak of them?
> Roar then, o roar, tremendous ocean!
> > Man, the ephemeral tyrant, he
> Busily in the dust builds future ruins,
> > But how should he command the sea? . . .

> > > > (*Essays, 349*)

The final poem written in Naples was composed in January 1820 as an inscription for the tomb of a little girl. It was written at the mother's request, and takes up a theme that haunted Batyushkov:

INSCRIPTION FOR THE TOMB OF MALISHEVA'S DAUGHTER

Dear friend who come here from my distant home,
I pray you: look upon this humble stone.

Two parents here have laid to rest their hope,
And I lie here in peace, their little one.
Report my words to them: "Dear ones, don't cry!
    Envy my ephemerality;
        I did not know this life,
        And know eternity."

(Essays, 350)

This little poem had an unexpected destiny. It was shown by Batyushkov's friend Bludov to the editor of the journal *Son of the Fatherland*, who took the liberty of publishing it without the author's consent or of course the consent of the woman who had asked for it. The poet's displeasure at this indiscreet behavior was one element in his rejection of the Russian literary establishment as he descended into mental illness.

■ □ ■

For health reasons, Batyushkov had himself transferred at the end of 1820 to Rome, where he had a more sympathetic superior. Soon, however, he was putting in official requests for retirement, and in May 1821, without waiting for an answer, he left Rome for Teplice, a spa town now in the Czech Republic, on the German border and close to the places where he and Petin had fought in 1807. He went there in search of a cure, bathing and taking the waters assiduously and cutting himself off from most Russian contacts. Even so, he was still interested in his literary work; in June he made marginal corrections on a copy of the *Essays* of 1817 with a view to a new edition—which never appeared. In this he proposed to omit some weaker pieces, replacing them with a new sequence consisting of six very short pieces in a similar vein to his translations from the Greek Anthology, but this time entirely original. They were virtually the last thing he wrote, and were not published until long after his death, in 1883, but they have been seen by many critics as his masterpiece.[5] With hindsight one can see them as marked by the crisis that Batyushkov was undergoing; they seem to be written less for conventional readers than for the poet himself. The third piece pursues the love theme that had dominated the Greek Anthology poems, but the rest are all concerned with life and death, courage and resignation. From a formal point of view, they are on a par with "You wake, o Baiae," but the melancholy beauty of the earlier poem is replaced in some of these with an excitingly unexpected choice of words and images, from the sun as "tsar of the azure desert" to the "crocodile waters" of life:

IMITATIONS OF THE ANCIENTS

I

Life without death's not life. What is it then? A bowl
    With a drop of honey in a sea of wormwood.
Magnificent the ocean! Azure king of the desert,
O sun, you are a wonder amid heaven's wonders!
    And there is so much beauty on the earth!
    Yet silver is all counterfeit and pointless.
    Weep, mortal, weep! Your earthly fortune
    Is in the hands of ruthless Nemesis.

II

    Mountains can feel the pull of music;
The camel is attentive to love's tune,
Groaning beneath his load; you see the rose

Blush deeper red than blood at songs
Of nightingales in valleys of the Yemen . . .
But you, my beauty . . . I don't understand.

III

Look how the cypress, like our steppe, is barren—
But always fresh and green.
Citizen, you can't bear fruit like the palm tree?
Then imitate the cypress;
Like it, alone and dignified and free.

IV

When a girl in agony is fading
And her body is blue and chilled,
It is in vain love pours out flowers
And amber; she must lie still,
Pale as a lily of the fields,
Like a waxen form; and now
Flowers cannot warm her cooling hands
And perfume has no power.

V

O mortal! Do you wish to go unharmed
Through the sea of life's commotion?
Do not be haughty; let the following wind
Spread your sail aloof and happy.

Don't quit the wheel when the fierce tempest roars!
Scipio when happy, Peter in life's storms.

VI

Do you want honey, son?—Never fear stings;
  The crown of victory?—Fight bravely!
Or is it pearls you long for?—Dive down deep
  Into the crocodile waters.
Fear not! God loves the brave; they are his own,
He keeps for them honey, pearls, death . . . a crown.

                                        (Essays, 351–52)

At about this time, Batyushkov became aware of the unautho-
rized publication of his epitaph for a little girl in *Son of the Father-
land*. This was swiftly followed in the same journal by a poem that
gave even greater offense. The culprit this time was the poet Pyotr
Pletnyov, a great admirer of Batyushkov, who without any malicious
intent wrote an epistle entitled "B . . . ov from Rome," where he
takes the liberty of speaking in the poet's name. It was published in
the journal anonymously, so that even some of his friends thought it
was by Batyushkov. It was not in itself particularly hurtful, but Baty-
ushkov, by this time feeling vulnerable and persecuted, took it very
badly—and Pletnyov, attempting to put things right, made the situ-
ation even worse by publishing in the same journal a brief and lau-
datory poem, "On a Portrait of Batyushkov." The poet, convinced
that Pletnyov was a stalking horse and complicit in a plot hatched
by unnamed enemies, dispatched an open letter to the editor of *Son
of the Fatherland*, declaring that he had given up writing and that
he was not a contributor to the journal. In fact this announcement,
which was sent by way of Gnedich, never appeared.

Batyushkov wrote again to Gnedich—for the last time—a few days later to explain his position as he saw it. Recognizing the value of his friend's work on the *Essays*, he declares, not quite accurately, that since its publication he has written nothing: "I promised myself that I would give up literature, at least with a view to publication, and I have kept this promise." Then came the business with *Son of the Fatherland* and "some person called Pletaev [sic]"—all of which filled him with indignation. He concludes:

> How can a person you don't know be so malevolent? I don't know, but it's plain to see. What did I do to deserve it? If Mr. Pletaev wrote verse under my name, why did the editors of *Son of the Fatherland* have to print it? No, I can't find words for my indignation: it will only die when I die. But the blow has been struck, and this is the consequence: I shall write no more, and I'll keep my word. Maybe I had a spark of talent; maybe with time I might have written something worthy of the public—I say it with pardonable pride—and worthy of myself, since I am 33 years old and six years of silence have made me not more foolish, but more mature. Things have turned out differently. I shall be a man without honor if ever I publish something in my name. What's more, insulted by praise, I have decided not to go back to Russia, since I fear people who, in spite of the fact that I shed my blood on the field of honor and am now in the service of my beloved monarch, use such an unworthy and base method of hurting me behind my back.
>
> (*SP*, 442–43)

This was Batyushkov's last surviving letter to any of his friends, and it marks the beginning of a steep decline. In the autumn of 1821 he moved to nearby Dresden and spent the winter there. His friends in Russia began to be seriously worried, having received alarming reports from his friend Bludov who had visited him in the summer; Aleksandr Turgenev wrote to Vyazemsky at the beginning of October: "Batyushkov is very depressed, he has fallen out with everybody, and according to Bludov he is on brink of the worst kind of melancholia" (*WP*, 287). Then, the following month, Zhukovsky, who had been traveling in the West, called to see him in a village near Dresden. His notebooks suggest that Batyushkov read aloud some poems, then tore them up, but one short but affecting poem does survive, a little piece written in Zhukovsky's album. The opening lines refer to Derzhavin's famous final lines about the river of life and death, then there is an allusion to loving sentiments expressed in Zhukovsky's own work, before the final obsessive return to poor Pletnyov, yet again transformed into Pletaev:

> Zhukovsky, time swallows everything,
> Both you and me, and fame and art,
> But what we cherish in our hearts
> Will not be drowned by oblivion.
> It cannot die, the heart, o no!
> Goodness outlasts the funeral bell . . .
> And what lives in your heart, I know,
> Not even Pletaev can tell.

(CP, 239)

After this, Batyushkov disappeared into silence during the Dresden winter, except that in December he wrote to the head of the diplomatic service, describing his situation in Naples and asking again to be allowed to retire from the service. Eventually he was given indefinite leave, and finally, contrary to what he had said to Gnedich, he reappeared in St. Petersburg. The story of his remaining tragic years can be quickly told.

INTO THE DARK

When he returned to St. Petersburg in March 1822, Batyushkov was nearly thirty-five years old; he had more than thirty-three years still to live. For all of this time he was disturbed, mentally ill, sometimes to the point of attempted suicide; for much of the time he was shut away, first in a clinic, then in houses belonging to family members, seeing little of his friends, and writing almost nothing—or at least nothing that has survived. What is usually seen as his last poem was composed some time between 1821 and 1824; it expresses the despair felt by Batyushkov at this time:

> Reader, have you not heard
> Of gray Melchisedec's last words?
> Man is born a slave,
> A slave goes to the grave,
> And can he hope that death will say
> Why he walked through this lovely vale of tears,
> Suffered, complained, accepted, disappeared?

> (*Essays, 353*)

Melchisedec is a priest mentioned in the book of Genesis. In the Epistle to the Hebrews (chapters 6 and 7), Christ is said to be "made an high priest for ever after the order of Melchisedec," and Melchisedec himself is described as a godlike figure, "without father, without mother, without descent, having neither beginning of days, nor end of life." There is nothing obvious to connect him with the bleak vision of Batyushkov's poem, which reminds one rather of the book of Job or Ecclesiastes ("for all his days are sorrows, and his travail grief")—but there seems no doubt that this composite prophetic figure speaks for the poet. Notice too that the "vale of tears" remains "lovely" (more literally, "miraculous"). The poem *might* have been written at about the same time as the "Imitations of the Ancients," and, dark as it is, it shares with them a formal perfection, a kind of gem-like beauty. A witness claimed to have seen it written in charcoal on the wall of Batyushkov's room at the end of his life.

When they saw him again in March 1822, his friends were alarmed at his condition; Karamzin wrote to Vyazemsky: "Batyushkov has come home a melancholic and a hypochondriac, gloomy and cold . . . he sits in his room and doesn't want to see us often" (*WP*, 291). But he was not without support. Until 1833, he was still officially in government service, although constantly on leave. This meant that the tsar's government took some responsibility for him, paying him a small salary, allowing him expenses for travel to a German clinic, overseeing his movements and dealing with arrangements for the management of his estate. His first desire on returning home was to set off again on his travels, this time to seek a cure in the Crimea, where he had once dreamed of settling with Anna Furman. He obtained the necessary passport, and disappeared from view, turning up in August in Simferopol, where he signed on with a celebrated psychiatrist. To no avail: during the winter his paranoiac condition worsened; he burned his books, tried more than once to kill himself, and had to be carefully watched. His old friend Vyazemsky commented (in a letter to Aleksandr Turgenev): "We are all born under some kind of disastrous constellation . . . Poor

Batyushkov, alone in an inn in Simferopol, devoured by the gloomy dreams of a disturbed imagination—that's a scene worthy of our Russian way of life and our epoch" (*WP*, 295).

Eventually he was brought back to the capital by force and lived there for the next year, refusing a room in his old home with the Muravyovs and preferring a little flat by himself. During this period he was assiduously cared for by his old Arzamas friends, particularly Turgenev, who often reported on his alarming condition to Vyazemsky in Moscow. There were relatively good days too, for instance May 17, of which Turgenev wrote: "Batyushkov is very depressed again . . . But yesterday we sat with him until one in the morning, and Bludov's jokes enlivened him and his wits. He joked with us about literary people and himself quoted some poems" (*WP*, 297). Overall, however, the prospects looked bleak, as Karamzin noted in a letter to Vyazemsky: "I saw Batyushkov, who was wearing a beard, and was in the most unhappy frame of mind: he talks nonsense about his illness and wants to hear of nothing else. I have no hope" (*WP*, 297). In April 1824, Batyushkov wrote a letter to the tsar requesting permission to retire to a monastery; the tsar's response was to have him sent to a specialist clinic at Sonnenstein, near Dresden.

Sonnenstein later became notorious as the site of a "National Socialist Death Institution," a precursor of the death camps; here the Nazis gassed those deemed unworthy of life, for the most part the mentally ill or the psychologically disabled. The same institution was in the early nineteenth century a very advanced center for the humane treatment of mental illness. Batyushkov spent four years there, from 1824 to 1828, accompanied by his devoted sister Aleksandra. At first he resisted treatment and tried to run away; later he became reconciled to the regime, but it did no good. He continued to be obsessed with the idea of a conspiracy against him. His state of mind can be seen in a letter, written to Zhukovsky in March 1826, referring to Batyushkov's superior, the foreign minister Nesselrode, who was responsible for having him sent to Sonnenstein:

> Slapped on the cheeks, tormented and accursed together with Martin Luther on the Sonnenstein machine by the insane Nesselrode, I have a consolation in God and the friendship of such people as you, Zhukovsky. I hope that Nesselrode will be punished as an assassin. I can never forgive him, neither I nor God nor decent, honest people. Comfort me with a visit; I await you impatiently in this place of penal servitude, where Batyushkov dies daily.
>
> *(WP, 300).*

He found some consolation in art, devoting himself to drawing and making wax models. His doctor, Anton Dietrich, left many accounts of this, noting that "he becomes so absorbed in drawing that he barely answers the questions the doctors ask him. Many of his finished drawings show real talent" (*WP*, 304). This talent is evident in earlier drawings, notably some vivid self-portraits, including one of the wounded Batyushkov on crutches in 1807. He continued to draw to the end of his life, often repeating the same landscape. Few of these drawings have survived, and none of the wax models, so we have to rely on Doctor Dietrich's notes, which indicate that he liked to draw Tasso in prison, and also to model his brother and sisters, his father, the tsar, Zhukovsky, and others. Nor had he entirely given up reading and writing. He remained faithful to Tasso, Chateaubriand, and Byron, even writing a letter addressed to "Lord Byron in England" two years after Byron's death.

As for his poetry, only one significant piece has survived from the years of his affliction, an "Imitation of Horace" sent in a letter to his nephew, Grigory Grevents, who looked after him in his final years, and to whose daughter Elizaveta the poem seems to be addressed. In the standard edition of his poems, this piece is relegated to the endnotes, where it is described as "a nonsensical collection of phrases," but it is worth more than this suggests. It is not so much an imitation of Horace as a parody of Derzhavin's poem "Monument," which is itself derived from Horace's famous "Exegi monumentum" (Odes III, 30)—also translated or imitated by Lomonosov and, later, Pushkin. All of these poets, taking stock of their achievements, proclaim the lasting value of what they have written—in Derzhavin's case:

> I have built myself a monument miraculous, eternal,
> Stronger than metal, higher than pyramids;
> Whirlwind and thunder will not overthrow it;
> It will not be destroyed by fleeting years.

Batyushkov follows the pattern, writing of his immortality as a poet, comparing himself with the tsar. His poem has its own strange logic, fascinatingly teased out by Ilya Kutik in an essay in the journal *Cardinal Points* (no. 5, 2015). Let me just add here that through all the absurdity Batyushkov's poetic gift is palpably present; this poem has something of the vigor and brilliance of his "Imitations of the Ancients," above all in the stunning, if puzzling, last line— here and in the preceding three lines I have felt free to follow the patterning of sound rather than the lexical meaning, which would translate more literally as: "Tsaritsas, rule as tsars, and you, the empress! / Tsars, do not rule as tsars, I myself am a tsar on Pindus! / Venus my sister, and you my little sister. / But my Caesar is the holy reaper (*a kesar' moy—svyatoy kosar'*)."

> I have built a huge, miraculous monument,
> Singing your praises: it will not see death!
> Like your sweet image, charming, benevolent
> (Witness Napoleon, our faithful friend)

I shan't see death. All I have done in letters,
Dodging oblivion will live in print.
Not Phoebus, I alone have forged these fetters
Where I can keep the universe shut in.
I was the first who dared to speak in Russian
Amusingly about Elise's virtue,
To chat with true simplicity of God
And thunder truth to tsars for their own good.
Be stars for us, my empress, my tsaritsas!
Tsars are not stars: Mount Pindus is *my* state,
Venus my sister, you my little sister,
    My Caesar—scissors in the hands of Fate.

                                       (CP, 323)

In the summer of 1827, Batyushkov was declared incurable and the following year he was sent back to St. Petersburg. He was accompanied by his faithful sister, Aleksandra, who not long afterward herself succumbed to mental illness and lived out her days alone in Khantonovo, much less well cared for than Konstantin. Another member of the party was the German Dr. Dietrich, who chose to stay with Batyushkov for all of two years, not really hoping for a cure, but wanting to make life easier for his patient. He was interested in poetry and translated poems by Zhukovsky, Vyazemsky, and Batyushkov himself, but above all he was a conscientious observer who left precious notes on the sick man's behavior. These are fascinating, though they make sorry reading; for instance in September 1828: "He would not allow them to light the stove in his room; they didn't obey him, and he opened the window, constantly repeating that Stackelberg, Nesselrode, and many others who would start tormenting him were all hiding in the stove." Or the following February: "This morning he begged Schultz to bring him a dagger for him to kill himself, since he's fed up of living; he had visions of

Vyazemsky, Zhukovsky, Tsar Aleksandr and others, all were writing down what he said and immediately sending it off somewhere" (*WP*, 329–30). In March 1830, he fell ill with pneumonia and was given up by his doctors. Friends came to see him before he died, including Pushkin, who tried in vain to talk to him; he had greatly admired Batyushkov since before their first meeting many years earlier, and this final meeting left a trace in his poem "God, let me not go mad . . .", where he also alludes to the poem "The Last Spring" (see chapter 5).[1] Against all expectations, Batyushkov recovered; he was to live another twenty-five years, for much of the time in better physical health than he had known in his more active days. But soon after his recovery, Dietrich gave up hope and returned to Germany, leaving his patient to friends and family.

There is tragically little to say about the last twenty-five years of the poet's life. In 1825, his brother-in-law P. A. Shipilov was given power of attorney to administer his estates, which he did very effectively, paying off many debts. In 1833, Batyushkov was finally allowed to retire from government service and was given a small pension; that same year his nephew Grigory Grevents took over the role of guardian and moved with him to his home town of Vologda. Thereafter, his life was quiet and outwardly uneventful. He lived on the upper floor of a town house, making some contact with neighbors and visitors and continuing to read and to draw a great deal. He loved seeing children. In the summer, he was often in a nearby village, where he spent many hours walking in the countryside, so that he remained strong and healthy in body. The artist N. V. Berg, who visited him in 1847, left a vivid description:

> His dark-gray eyes were mobile and expressive, with a quiet, gentle look. His thick eyebrows, black with a touch of grey, were neither lowered nor contracted. However hard I looked, I could see no sign of madness in his modest, noble face. . . . His whole face was thin,

somewhat wrinkled and remarkable for its extraordinary mobility. It moved like lightning, with rapid transitions from quietness to uneasiness, from smiles to severity. In general he is very lively and even restless. Everything he does, he does quickly. He walks quickly too, taking big strides.

(WP, 338)

As the years passed, he seems to have become less agitated, though still unpredictable and strange in his opinions. Witnesses noted his quietness, his politeness, particularly to women, his love of children and flowers, his desire to dress well, his taste for the theatre. He even began to be interested in the newspapers, especially at the time of the Crimean War (just before his death), so much so that his old bugbear and admirer Pletnyov wrote to Vyazemsky in January 1855: "Batyushkov has suddenly come to himself again, and hearing about the siege of Sebastopol, asked people to collect as many maps as possible of the place; since then he has been much engaged in European politics. That's what can be called rising up from the grave, having lain there for thirty years" (*WP*, 339).

Talk of resurrection was premature; in July of that year, Batyushkov died of typhus, a quiet death followed by a well-attended funeral and burial in a monastery not far from Vologda. He had written almost nothing for many years—or if he did, it has not survived, with one small exception, a poem dated May 14, 1853, entitled "Inscription for a Portrait of Count Bukshoevden of Sweden and Finland. And Also for an Image of Khvostov-Suvorov." Bukshoevden commanded the Russian forces during the Swedish campaign of 1808–1809, in which Batyushkov had taken part; Dmitry Khvostov was a much-mocked poet of the Shishkov camp and married to a daughter of General Suvorov. Why Batyushkov linked them to this poem is anyone's guess:

I'm very strangely made—as you'll agree:
　　I can both yawn and sneeze,
　　I wake only to sleep
And sleep to wake eternally.

(*CP, 323*)

■ □ ■

In 1853, a couple of years before Batyushkov died, his old friend Pyotr Vyazemsky, now transformed from irreverent young wit to serious conservative politician, was on holiday in Germany. Taking a trip on the Elbe near Dresden, he found himself close to the psychiatric clinic where his fellow poet had spent four years nearly thirty years before. Memories of the sick Batyushkov came flooding back. His poem entitled "Sonnenstein" begins with two stanzas about the beauties of the region before calling up the melancholy past and the still more melancholy present of his friend:

Enchanted country, full of light, then somber,
You living keepsake of the lovely world,
It was beyond your power to lift and scatter
The cloud of thought that settled on my soul.

It was a different vision held me captive,
A charming image visited my soul,
That suffering image, like a grieving shadow,
Hid nature's beauty under a dark pall.

He suffered here, here for a time he languished,
Zhukovsky's dearest bosom friend and mine,
In song and suffering our own Torquato
Who saw his sun set long before he died.

Not for his eyes did nature bud and flower,
Her sacred voice fell silent where he stood,
And here the clear blue skies could not awaken
The warmth of happy days in his sad blood.

His inner world was one of nightmare visions,
Locked in himself, as in a prison cell,
His mind shuttered against outward impressions,
God's world for him was like a lightless hell.

But what he saw, what caused his mind to tremble,
Was what disease engendered in that mind,
And here, poor man, he lived out years of suffering
And still he lives, our godforsaken friend.[2]

Without having died, the sick man was dead to the outside world. Much earlier, some time in 1822, Vyazemsky had written down in his notebooks what Batyushkov had said about his writing: "What can I write, what can I say about my poems? . . . I am like a man who didn't reach his goal and was carrying on his head a beautiful vessel full of something. The vessel slipped from his head, fell and was shattered into smithereens. Just try guessing what was in it!" (*SP*, 448). And indeed his legacy must be seen as incomplete; heaven knows what he might have written if his life had turned out better. But then the same can be said of Lermontov, of Keats, of many others, and like them, in spite of everything, Batyushkov achieved a great deal in relatively few years. Quite apart from the intrinsic value of his prose and verse, he was one of the principal creators of Russian Golden Age poetry, building on his reading and translation of foreign poetry, ancient and modern, to forge a fluent, natural-seeming, yet richly sonorous language for the expression of emotion, experience, and imagination. He also provided some of the first examples for a whole range of literary genres: elegy, poetic epistle, lighthearted literary satire, the short "anthological poem," the letter to friends, the sketch of daily life, art criticism.

Naturally then, Batyushkov became—and remained—a pivotal figure in Russian literary history, although literary historians have an unfortunate tendency to see him above all as a precursor of Aleksandr Pushkin. Undoubtedly Pushkin did learn a lot from Batyushkov, as well as going beyond him in many ways, but the older poet should be read for his own value rather than as a precious influence. His *Essays in Prose and Verse* were twice reissued under different titles before the poet's death, but the essential edition of his works by L. N. Maykov was published in 1885–1887, in three volumes. It may be this recent publication that prompted Chekhov, in his 1889 play *The Wood Demon* (and later in the closely related *Uncle Vanya*), to have his tedious professor Serebryakov ask his young wife Elena to fetch a Batyushkov volume that he thinks he has in his library. By this stage Batyushkov was probably not widely read by the general public, so the professor's request very likely signifies an out-of-touch academic attitude.

There are quite different and entirely positive mentions of Batyushkov some forty years later in the works of a poet who was the opposite of a dry-as-dust professor, Osip Mandelstam. I quoted in the introduction his eloquent poetic greeting to his distant predecessor; there are also two mentions of Batyushkov in his prose writings on poetry. In "Notes on Poetry," written in 1923, he declares: "Only those who were directly involved in the great secularization of the Russian language, in making it the language of the laity, helped to accomplish the task of primary significance in the development of Russian poetry. These include Trediakovsky, Lomonosov, Batyushkov, Yazykov, and most recently Khlebnikov and Pasternak." And following up on this the same year in "Storm and Stress," he again sets Batyushkov alongside Pasternak, remarking of the latter's new collection *My Sister Life*: "So new and so mature a harmony has not sounded in Russian poetry since the days of Batyushkov."[3]

Nearer our own times, Batyushkov lives again in a remarkable verse novel by Maria Rybakova, *Gnedich* (2011).[4] Centered on Gnedich and his translation of Homer, this is also much concerned with the friendship that has figured so largely in the present book, citing letters between the friends and evoking themes from Batyushkov's work. I have been inspired by *Gnedich* to complete my study of his friend. But I should like to finish this book with another verse tribute to the poet and his tragic fate, an elusive and moving poem that remained with me as I read and translated Batyushkov. It is the work of the Chuvash-Russian poet, Gennady Aygi (1934–2006);[5] the epigraph is taken from the poem by Vyazemsky just quoted:

House of the Poet in Vologda
(Konstantin Batyushkov)

A charming image visited my soul . . . (P. Vyazemsky)

but alongside—a surrounding of silk:
torn as if in a mixture

of his shining
and the trembling:

unceasing: of the temple—

altering the face
as in wind—

in shining of silk—as of features

of dust!—

of everything:

that is—

corroded by wind from the windows:

and by light: to the living face—

concealing itself
like a treasure:

amidst the silk:

the wind:

and the rays

1966

NOTES

INTRODUCTION

1. *Poems of Osip Mandelstam,* trans. Peter France (New York: New Directions, 2014), 51.
2. For a list of the sources used for the present volume see the abbreviations list (p. xi) in the front matter.

1. VOLOGDA TO ST. PETERSBURG

1. Gavrila Derzhavin (1743–1816), born near Kazan in modern Tatarstan, was the outstanding Russian poet of the late eighteenth century and an influential figure at the court of Catherine the Great. He is best known for his grand odes and his powerfully original style.
2. In the poem "At Tsarskoe Selo" (1911) in her first collection, *Evening.*
3. Cited in a note to the poem in *CP,* 314.
4. "Sentimentalist," a standard term in Russian literary history, has no pejorative overtones, referring to a new proto-Romantic sensibility that owed something to Sterne's *Sentimental Journey.*
5. "Must one [you] be so fickle, / I said to sweet pleasure." Madame de Murat was a now largely forgotten French poet of the seventeenth century.
6. See Peter France, "Fingal in Russia," in *The Reception of Ossian in Europe,* ed. Howard Gaskill (London: Thoemmes Continuum, 2004), 259–73.
7. "What do I see, it is over, I embrace you, and you die."

2. WAR AND PEACE

1. Bread and salt are the traditional Russian expression of hospitality.
2. Don Quixote's worn-out steed; a literal translation of the original is "magnificent nag."

3. François-René de Chateaubriand, *Historical Essay on Revolutions* (Essai historique sur les révolutions), book 1, part 1, chap. 22.

4. Nikolay Gavrilovich Kurganov (1725–1796), a mathematician and academician, was the author of an influential Russian grammar that included an anthology of poetry.

5. See *The Penguin Book of Russian Poetry*, ed. Robert Chandler, Boris Dralyuk, and Irina Mashinski (London: Penguin, 2015), 17.

3. THE CITY AND THE COUNTRY

1. Crates of Thebes, a Cynical philosopher of the fourth century BCE.

2. See his biographical note in *An Age Ago: A Selection of Nineteenth-Century Russian Poetry*, selected and translated by Alan Myers with a foreword and biographical notes by Joseph Brodsky (London: Penguin, 1989). This volume contains four translations of poems by Batyushkov.

3. Yevgeny Baratynsky, *Half-light and Other Poems*, trans. Peter France (Todmorden: Arc, 2015), 18–21.

4. Mikhail Kachenovsky (1775–1842), conservative critic, associated with the journal Moscow Herald (*Vestnik moskvy*).

5. Ermil Kostrov (1755–1796), translator of Homer and Ossian.

6. Aleksey Kruchonykh (1886–1967) declared that his "transrational" text "Dyr bul shchyl" was more Russian than all of Pushkin.

7. "My health is fleeing; this unfaithful one / Makes no promise to return, / And Nature who is tottering / Has already warned me / Not to count too much on her. / So the play will suddenly end / With the second act: / Quickly I reach the denouement, / The curtain falls and I am forgotten."

8. "In her age of beauty, the flower of youth . . . / . . . Gone up to heaven, alive and beautiful"

4. BACK TO WAR

1. General A. N. Bakhmetev, a wounded war hero who was soon to become Batyushkov's commanding officer.

2. *War and Peace*, vol. 3, part 1, chap. 12.

3. The form and imagery of this poem inspired Pushkin's first major composition, "Reminiscences in Tsarskoe Selo," which the young student famously read aloud before Derzhavin on January 8, 1815.

5. THE RETURN OF ODYSSEUS

1. Compare the lines from "The Bronze Horseman":

   We'll build a city here, a port,
   To challenge our disdainful neighbors . . .
   A hundred years have passed since then;
   a northern city, young, a wonder,
   has, from the forest and the fen,
   risen in majesty and splendor

   (*Penguin Book of Russian Poetry, 88*)

2. The halcyon, also referred to in "Shade of a Friend," is a bird from Greek mythology, reputed to build its nest on quiet waters—whence the expression "halcyon days."
3. Baratynsky, *Half-light*, 100–101.
4. Aleksandr Pushkin, "To Batyushkov" (1815). The quotation is taken from the first of two similar poems with the same title.

6. ARZAMAS AND THE *ESSAYS*

1. Not related to the novelist Ivan Turgenev, who was more than thirty years his junior.
2. Sergey Sokovnin (1785–1868) was an amateur poet who had distinguished himself by declaring publicly on the street his love for Vyazemsky's wife. Nikolay Ilyin (1777–1823), a dramatist and translator, was a member of the Society of Lovers of Literature.
3. " . . . And like a swift Alpine torrent, / Like a flash of lightning / In the clear night sky, / Like a breeze or smoke, / Or like a sudden arrow, / Our fame flies past: and every honor / Is like a fragile flower. /

   What do you hope for, or what do you now expect? / After the triumph and the palms / All that remains for the soul/Is grief and lamentations and tearful complaints. / What help can come from love or from friendship henceforth! / O tears! O sorrow! (Torquato Tasso, *Torrismondo*).
4. See *After Lermontov: Translations for the Bicentenary*, ed. Peter France and Robyn Marsack (Manchester: Carcanet, 2014), 128–41.

7. TO ITALY

1. "Your value increases when people listen to you."
2. "And that's how they write history."
3. "Do you know the land where the lemon trees flower?"—the first line of Mignon's song in Goethe's *Wilhelm Meister*.
4. Ilya Serman notes: "Later, critics came to consider these 'anthological' verses of Batyushkov's his highest achievement. Belinsky [the major Russian critic of the nineteenth century] thought them 'the best product of his muse.'" According to Belinsky, these poems are distinguished by "simplicity, unity of thought capable of expression in a small space, directness and loftiness of tone, plasticity and grace of form." See Ilya Sermain, *Konstantin Batyushkov* (New York: Twayne, 1974), 142.
5. For instance, D. S. Mirsky writes: "For strange beauty and haunting emotional intensity they are unique in Russian poetry. They are a rare instance of the creative influence of mental illness on poetry." *A History of Russian Literature*, ed. and abr. Francis J. Whitfield (London: Routledge and Kegan Paul, 1949), 78.

8. INTO THE DARK

1. On this allusion see Nabokov's comments in *Eugene Onegin: A Novel in Verse*, by Aleksandr Pushkin, translated from the Russian with a commentary by Vladimir Nabokov, revised edition (London: Routledge and Kegan Paul, 1975), vol. 3, 74.
2. P. A. Vyazemsky, *Selected Works* (Izbrannye sochineniya), ed. V. S. Nechaeva (Moscow/Leningrad: Academia, 1935), 267–68.
3. Osip Mandelstam, *The Collected Critical Prose and Letters*, ed. Jane Gary Harris (London: Harper Collins, 1991), 166, 179.
4. Translated into English under the same title by Elena Dimov (Tilburg, Netherlands: Glagoslav, 2015).
5. See Gennady Aygi, *Selected Poems, 1954–1994*, bilingual edition, trans. Peter France (London: Angel Books, 1997), 64–65. A slightly earlier poem, "Ever more often—Batyushkov," is included in Aygi's *Winter Revels*, trans. Peter France (San Francisco: Rumor Books, 2009), 28.

TRANSLATOR'S NOTE

This volume contains, in whole or in part, rather more than half of Batyushkov's poetic output. These translated poems are at the heart of this book, so I should say a few words here about what Walter Benjamin called the "task of the translator." The translation of poetry has called forth many dogmatic pronouncements (including those of Benjamin). Many of the arguments concern questions of prosody, which are posed in a particularly acute way by Russian poetry. Batyushkov, like his contemporaries and many of his successors, placed great value on form. His work explores the possibilities of metre and rhyme in many different genres, ranging from the familiar verse letter to the formal elegy. All of his poems use rhyme, generally with an alternation of masculine and feminine endings, and sometimes in quite complicated stanzas, and he was renowned among contemporaries for the sonorous beauty of his language. Clearly it is impossible to reproduce all this directly in a translation, but one can seek to create English poems that point to specific qualities of the Russian originals. In a word, these are not free versions inspired in some way by the Russian poems, but *close* translations. I generally translate line for line (though with some transpositions), and I try not to omit or replace what I see as the essential elements of meaning. The Russian metres are sometimes modified: for instance, lines of twelve syllables may be replaced by lines of ten, since Russian words tend to have more syllables than English ones. Almost always, however, I attempt to suggest the *rhythms* of the Russian poems, including in many cases the masculine and feminine endings. Rhyme is particularly tricky; like most English-language translators, I avoid the full rhyming that characterizes most Russian poetry, but generally try to preserve the rhyming principle with a variety of slant rhymes, alliterations, assonances, and the like. I hope enough of Batyushkov's voice (or rather his many voices) will come across for the reader to see why I have taken on this daunting but (for me) irresistible task.

INDEX OF TEXTS BY BATYUSHKOV CITED OR DISCUSSED

PROSE (NOT INCLUDING PRIVATE LETTERS)